I0015346

Windows Terminal Tips, Tricks, and Productivity Hacks

Optimize your command-line usage and development processes with pro-level techniques

Will Fuqua

BIRMINGHAM—MUMBAI

Windows Terminal Tips, Tricks, and Productivity Hacks

Copyright © 2021 Packt Publishing

All rights reserved. No part of this book may be reproduced, stored in a retrieval system, or transmitted in any form or by any means, without the prior written permission of the publisher, except in the case of brief quotations embedded in critical articles or reviews.

Every eff ort has been made in the preparation of this book to ensure the accuracy of the information presented. However, the information contained in this book is sold without warranty, either express or implied. Neither the author, nor Packt Publishing or its dealers and distributors, will be held liable for any damages caused or alleged to have been caused directly or indirectly by this book.

Packt Publishing has endeavored to provide trademark information about all of the companies and products mentioned in this book by the appropriate use of capitals. However, Packt Publishing cannot guarantee the accuracy of this information.

Associate Group Product Manager: Pavan Ramchandani

Publishing Product Manager: Kaustubh Manglurkar

Senior Editor: Sofi Rogers

Content Development Editor: Aamir Ahmed

Technical Editor: Saurabh Kadave

Copy Editor: Safis Editing

Project Coordinator: Ajesh Devavaram

Proofreader: Safis Editing

Indexer: Tejal Daruwale Soni

Production Designer: Jyoti Chauhan

First published: April 2021

Production reference: 1280421

Published by Packt Publishing Ltd.
Livery Place
35 Livery Street
Birmingham
B3 2PB, UK.

ISBN 978-1-80020-756-1

www.packt.com

To my kind and loving wife, Koi, who showed the utmost patience during the writing of this book.

– Will

Foreword

Whether you are building a web app or working in the cloud, the command line has always been an integral tool for software developers and IT admins alike. For many years, the Windows command-line experience lagged behind that of Unix-based systems. Even simple things, such as selecting and copying text, required you to jump through hoops.

In the 2010s, Microsoft began to improve the command-line experience with Windows Subsystem for Linux (WSL), PowerShell improvements, and a command-line interface. WSL provided a first-party solution to running a Linux environment on your Windows device. PowerShell continued to receive incremental improvements to surpass the usability of CMD. The Windows Package Manager released a command-line interface as a first-party solution to install software on your machine. Even with all of these command-line tools, Windows lacked a solid terminal to host them in and Microsoft quickly realized how difficult it was to make improvements without breaking certain legacy behavior.

In 2019, Microsoft introduced the Windows Terminal, a new unified experience for hosting command-line tools. To make things better, Windows Terminal was open sourced alongside the in-box console host experience with which Windows command-line users were already familiar. It put customizability first, with a profile-based settings model and key bindings. Furthermore, a rapid release cycle helped to collect and address user feedback swiftly.

This book does a fantastic job of teaching you how to set up Windows Terminal and make it your own. You will learn how to create and manage your profiles to get the most out of your terminal and customize your actions and key bindings to be an effective user. Even better, you will learn how to get started using the terminal more often in day-to-day activities. The author teaches you how to use PowerShell and bash and how to customize them for your needs. The book will also teach you how to apply these tools to build apps, manage remote systems, and interact with the cloud.

Carlos Zamora

Software Engineer on Windows Terminal at Microsoft

Contributors

About the author

Will Fuqua has been developing software professionally for 12 years using a wide range of technologies. Initially based in the United States as a software consultant, he developed production systems for companies in the healthcare and finance industries, among many others. He then moved abroad and is now the Head of Engineering for an online travel agency, where he leads a high-powered technology team out of Bangkok, Thailand. You can find him online at `https://fuqua.io/`.

About the reviewers

Chester Liu is an open source enthusiast living in China. He got his first job as an iOS developer in 2016, after he graduated from college. During his professional career, he has worked on various platforms and in different areas. He is a long-time member of the GitHub community and has been contributing to the Windows Terminal project since 2019, after the project was open sourced by Microsoft. His contribution to the project falls into different areas, including, but not limited to, rendering, performance, and VT support.

I'd like to thank the core team of the Console subsystem at Microsoft, who I'm glad to have made acquaintance with through our collaboration in the Windows Terminal project. They went through the trouble of convincing the management to open source a deep OS component of the Windows OS itself, just to bring the community a thrilling console experience. At the end of the day, the members of the console team are the ones who dived into the legacy console source code and have been trying to improve the console experience on Windows for the past several years. Dustin L. Howett, the tech leader of the console team, is one of the coolest tech leaders I know, and I'm truly honored to be a member of his "external" team.

Daniel Engberg is a principal consultant and partner at Agdiwo, an IT services company based in Gothenburg, Sweden. Daniel's focus is Microsoft enterprise client management, including Microsoft Endpoint Configuration Manager (formerly System Center Configuration Manager), Windows 10, and PowerShell.

Daniel has been writing on his blog since 2010 and is active on Twitter.

Table of Contents

3
Configuring an Ubuntu Linux profile

Section 2: Configuring your Windows Terminal and its shells

4
Customizing your Windows Terminal settings

5
Changing your Windows Terminal appearance

6

Setting up keyboard shortcuts

7

Hidden Windows Terminal Actions

8

Tips for using PowerShell like a Pro

9
Tips for Using Ubuntu like an Expert

Section 3: Using your Windows Terminal for development

10
Using Git and GitHub with Windows Terminal

11
Building web applications with React

12
Building REST APIs with C# and Windows Terminal

13
Connecting to remote systems

14
Managing systems in the cloud

Appendix
Windows Terminal Actions

Other Books You May Enjoy

Index

Preface

Windows Terminal is a modern and open source command-line program for Windows 10, built for Command Prompt, PowerShell, **Windows Subsystem for Linux (WSL2)**, and more. It's fast and flexible, but to use it effectively we need to understand both Windows Terminal and the shells that run inside it. We'll explore these technologies in detail throughout the three sections of this book.

We'll start by covering the benefits of Windows Terminal, including its GPU-accelerated rendering and JSON-based configurability. We'll learn how to use and customize the built-in tabs, panes, and key bindings to drive our own beautiful and efficient terminal workflows.

Next, we'll show how to use PowerShell Core and the Windows Subsystem for Linux within Windows Terminal. We'll maximize our productivity using powerful tools such as PSReadLine on PowerShell and ZSH on Linux, and pick up some time-saving tricks for common developer tools such as Git and SSH.

Finally, we'll see how Windows Terminal can be used in common development and DevOps tasks, such as developing frontend JavaScript applications and backend REST APIs and controlling Amazon Web Services, Azure, and Google Cloud.

By the end of this book, we'll not only be experts on Windows Terminal, but we'll also know how to use shells such as PowerShell Core and ZSH to become proficient through the command line.

Who this book is for

This book is for developers, DevOps engineers, and sysadmins who want to become advanced command-line power users. Whether you're new to the command line or you use PowerShell every day, this book will have something for you.

What this book covers

This book covers Windows Terminal up to version 1.7, and comprises the following chapters.

Section 1 – Introducing the New Windows Terminal

Chapter 1, Getting started with the new Windows Terminal, discusses how Windows Terminal works with existing shells such as PowerShell, cmd.exe, and the Windows Subsystem for Linux. It discusses the speed, configurability, and open source development of Windows Terminal, and how to install, update, and launch it.

Chapter 2, Learning the Windows Terminal UI, covers how to use Windows Terminal's tabs, manage terminal panes, and open different shells, including PowerShell and cmd.exe. Relevant hotkeys are mentioned wherever applicable and useful. This chapter covers all the major parts of Windows Terminal's UI.

Chapter 3, Configuring an Ubuntu Linux profile, gives an overview of the benefits of the **Windows Subsystem For Linux** (**WSL2**), guides you through setting up a WSL2 Ubuntu system, and shows how to launch it as a Windows Terminal profile. It also discusses how to access Windows from Linux, and vice versa.

Section 2 – Configuring your Windows Terminal and its shells

Chapter 4, Customizing your Windows Terminal settings, covers the settings.json file and the settings UI. It guides you through the overall structure and editing of this file and covers a number of useful settings to enable in Windows Terminal.

Chapter 5, Changing your Windows Terminal appearance, shows how to tweak the appearance of Windows Terminal to make it both beautiful and more functional. It broadly has two parts: customizing Windows Terminal itself and then customizing the shells to match.

Chapter 6, Setting up keyboard shortcuts, covers the basics of Windows Terminal's command/key binding system, and recommends some additional key bindings to set.

Chapter 7, Hidden Windows Terminal Actions, details the many commands that are hidden by default—that is, unbound and inaccessible until they're mapped to keyboard shortcuts in the settings. This chapter covers some of the more practical hidden key bindings, such as "focus mode" and "pin on top."

Chapter 8, Tips for using PowerShell like a Pro, focuses on using PowerShell as an interactive shell in Windows Terminal. It shows some time-saving tips and tricks for accomplishing tasks quickly and effortlessly.

Chapter 9, Tips for using Ubuntu like an Expert, covers how to use WSL2 Ubuntu with Windows. Additionally, this chapter shares a selection of useful tips for configuring WSL2 Ubuntu in Windows Terminal to provide a richer and more productive environment.

Section 3 – Using your Windows Terminal for development

Chapter 10, Using Git and GitHub with Windows Terminal, contains tips and tricks for using Git and GitHub quickly and efficiently. It covers both the initial setup and the installation of these systems, as well as workflow optimization tools such as **gh**.

Chapter 11, Building web applications with React, covers how to build a frontend React application inside WSL2 using Windows Terminal and VS Code. It focuses on efficient workflows when using Windows Terminal for frontend development.

Chapter 12, Building REST APIs with C# and Windows Terminal, shows how to build a simple web API using .NET. It details various Windows Terminal pane layouts for running the application, continuously testing, and experimenting with C#.

Chapter 13, Connecting to remote systems, introduces both WinRM and SSH. It uses SSH to connect remotely to both Windows and Linux systems, and provides useful tips on how to create a streamlined setup for connecting to frequently used remote machines.

Chapter 14, Managing systems in the cloud, covers setting up Azure Cloud Shell and Google Cloud Shell in Windows Terminal, and additionally covers the Amazon Web Services command line for administering cloud systems.

To get the most out of this book

To get the most out of this book, you'll need a relatively up-to-date version of Windows 10. The minimum required version is Windows 10 version 1903 (build 18362), which was released in May 2019. Some of the more advanced features in this book will require a more up-to-date version. Any chapter that requires a more up-to-date version will make this clear at the beginning of the chapter.

If you are using the digital version of this book, we advise you to type any code or configuration options yourself or access the code via the GitHub repository (link available in the next section). Doing so will help you avoid any potential errors related to copying and pasting from PDFs or ebook readers.

Download the example configuration and code files

You can download the example configuration and code for this book from GitHub at `https://github.com/PacktPublishing/Windows-Terminal-Tips-Tricks-and-Productivity-Hacks`. In case there's an update to the code, it will be updated on the existing GitHub repository.

We also have other code bundles from our rich catalog of books and videos available at `https://github.com/PacktPublishing/`. Check them out!

Download the color images

We also provide a PDF file that has color images of the screenshots/diagrams used in this book. You can download it here: `https://static.packt-cdn.com/downloads/9781800207561_ColorImages.pdf`

Conventions used

There are a number of text conventions used throughout this book.

`Code in text`: Indicates code words in text, configuration files, folder names, filenames, file extensions, and program names. Here is an example: "To ping the server, run `ping example.com` from the terminal."

A block of code is set as follows:

```
{
    "command": "togglePaneZoom",
    "keys": "alt+shift+z"
}
```

When we wish to draw your attention to a particular part of a code block, the relevant lines or items are set in bold:

```
{
    "command": "togglePaneZoom",
    "keys": "alt+shift+z"
}
```

Any command-line input or output is written as follows:

```
mkdir my-project
cd my-project
```

Bold: Indicates a new term, an important word, or words that you see onscreen. For example, words in menus or dialog boxes appear in the text like this. Here is an example: "Select **System info** from the **Administration** panel."

> **Tips or important notes**
> Appear like this.

Get in touch

Feedback from our readers is always welcome.

General feedback: If you have questions about any aspect of this book, mention the book title in the subject of your message and email us at customercare@packtpub.com.

Errata: Although we have taken every care to ensure the accuracy of our content, mistakes do happen. If you have found a mistake in this book, we would be grateful if you would report this to us. Please visit www.packtpub.com/support/errata, selecting your book, clicking on the Errata Submission Form link, and entering the details.

Piracy: If you come across any illegal copies of our works in any form on the Internet, we would be grateful if you would provide us with the location address or website name. Please contact us at copyright@packt.com with a link to the material.

If you are interested in becoming an author: If there is a topic that you have expertise in and you are interested in either writing or contributing to a book, please visit authors.packtpub.com.

Reviews

Please leave a review. Once you have read and used this book, why not leave a review on the site that you purchased it from? Potential readers can then see and use your unbiased opinion to make purchase decisions, we at Packt can understand what you think about our products, and our authors can see your feedback on their book. Thank you!

For more information about Packt, please visit packt.com.

Section 1:
Introducing the New
Windows Terminal

In this section, we'll learn to make efficient use of Windows Terminal. We'll start out learning about what Windows Terminal is and why it's interesting, and then quickly move on to installing and using it. We'll cover all the user interface components of Windows Terminal, including tabs, panes, and the profile menu. We'll also set up an Ubuntu profile using WSL2, so we'll have functioning PowerShell, cmd.exe, and Ubuntu profiles ready to use!

This section comprises the following chapters:

- *Chapter 1, Getting started with the new Windows Terminal*
- *Chapter 2, Learning the Windows Terminal UI*
- *Chapter 3, Configuring an Ubuntu Linux profile*

1

Getting started with the new Windows Terminal

At the Build 2019 conference, Microsoft made an exciting announcement: Windows 10 was getting a brand new command-line terminal! Custom built for the command prompt, PowerShell, and the Windows Subsystem for Linux, this new terminal promised to bring a modern, configurable, and open source command-line experience. In May 2020, Microsoft released the 1.0 version of the new Windows Terminal.

Windows Terminal is a separate application from the old Windows command line. This approach allows both terminals to live side by side, and enables Microsoft to rapidly release new features for Windows Terminal without endangering the backward compatibility of the old terminal.

By the end of this chapter, we will be up and running with Windows Terminal, having covered the following topics:

- Why a new terminal?
- The modern foundations of Windows Terminal
- Installing Windows Terminal
- Launching Windows Terminal

We'll cover why Windows needed a new terminal at all, how this new terminal is radically different from the old one, and take our first steps to download, install, and launch it.

Technical requirements

To get started with Windows Terminal, you'll need a Windows 10 installation with access to the built-in Microsoft Store application. The minimum version of Windows 10 supported is the May 2019 Update (version 1903, as reported in the output of the `winver` command). If you have a relatively up-to-date Windows 10 installation, you have all the tools you need to get started.

Why a new terminal?

Microsoft's old terminal, `conhost.exe`, has been showing its age. While it has seen some impressive improvements lately, such as ANSI/VT support and advanced settings, the primary goal of `conhost.exe` is to be backward-compatible with older applications. This backward-compatibility constraint can sometimes be at odds with the fast-paced improvements in other parts of Windows 10.

While both PowerShell and the shells running under **Windows Subsystem for Linux (WSL)** have been seeing constant, rapid improvement, the "user experience" of the Windows command line was in vast need of an upgrade, when compared to its macOS and GNU/Linux counterparts.

As we're getting started, it's useful to understand the difference between a **terminal** and a **shell**. A **terminal** is essentially "what you see" when using the command line—it renders the text, draws any **user interface** (**UI**) widgets, and accepts keyboard and mouse input. The terminal will then send this input to the shell for processing. The old terminal on Windows was called `conhost.exe` and was the only built-in terminal; however, there were and still are alternative third-party terminals such as ConEmu and Hyper.

A **shell** doesn't have a UI; it's a command-line program that receives input from the terminal, evaluates that input, and returns the result. Shells, such as the command prompt, PowerShell, and those running in WSL, require a terminal to collect input and display output. Launching the cmd.exe or powershell.exe shells from the Start menu or Run dialog will implicitly start the conhost.exe terminal, which can make the distinction less obvious for end users:

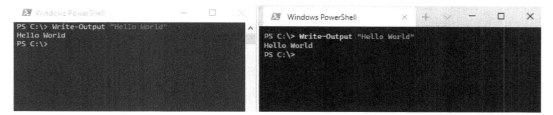

Figure 1.1 – PowerShell, running in both the old conhost on the left, and the new Windows Terminal on the right

This delineation between terminals and shells means that switching to the new Windows Terminal is painless—the shells, such as the command prompt and PowerShell, are not changing. All existing knowledge and documentation of the command prompt, PowerShell, and shells under WSL can be reused, but commands will be sent through the new, more powerful Windows Terminal instead of the older, more barebones conhost. exe. Let's see what makes this new Windows Terminal so much better!

> **Note**
>
> A more in-depth discussion about the differences between shells and terminals can be found on Scott Hanselman's blog at https://www.hanselman.com/blog/whats-the-difference-between-a-console-a-terminal-and-a-shell.

The modern foundations of Windows Terminal

Earlier, we learned that Windows Terminal is built from the ground up to provide a more modern and flexible command-line experience. This command-line experience has three main parts: a modern UI, a flexible JSON-based customization system, and its open source development.

A Modern UI

When working with the command line, it's common to have a couple of command lines open. Perhaps a couple of operations need to be monitored at the same time, or some commands need to execute in PowerShell, and others need to use WSL. In the old terminal, the only option is to open separate windows and then *Alt + Tab* between them.

The new Windows Terminal comes with multiple options for managing these tasks. It features built-in tab support, each tab with its own shell, and all available within the same window:

Figure 1.2 – The new Windows Terminal with multiple shells open in tabs

Additionally, some operations work best with multiple shells open side by side. The old terminal again had no support for this; the only option was to use separate windows positioned next to each other. The new Windows Terminal supports "panes" that can open multiple different shells within the same tab. It's not just limited to two panes, either—the terminal supports multiple side-by-side panes split both vertically and horizontally:

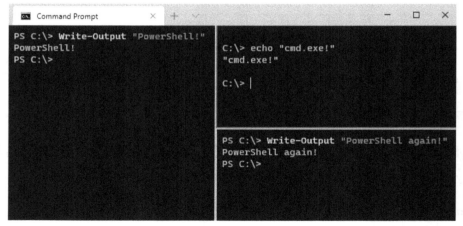

Figure 1.3 – The new Windows Terminal with multiple shells open in a single tab

We'll dive more into efficient tab and pane management in *Chapter 2, Learning the Windows Terminal UI.*

Improved visual effects

The modern UI features are not just limited to tabs and panes; the entire terminal has been written from the ground up to take advantage of the latest technology. The terminal itself is written using the **Universal Windows Platform** (**UWP**) framework with XAML Islands, and text rendering is handled by a GPU-accelerated rendering engine using DirectX.

This technology stack, in addition to being a flexible, fast, and solid foundation, enables improved visual effects as well. For example, the new Windows Terminal natively supports transparency using an effect called acrylic, as well as background images and GIFs:

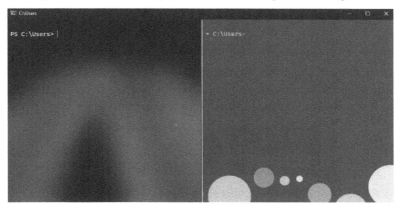

Figure 1.4 – Left pane: PowerShell with the acrylic transparency effect. Right pane: cmd with a background image

Improved fonts and rendering

The new, GPU-accelerated rendering engine has all the modern features expected for a first-class command-line experience. The GPU acceleration results in ultra-fast and crisp text rendering, and the new rendering engine enables Unicode character support. While full, multi-language Unicode support is still a work in progress, the foundation is laid.

To show off the new Windows Terminal's font-rendering capabilities, Microsoft released a brand-new open source programming font named Cascadia Code, which is bundled in Windows Terminal:

```
The new Cascadia Code Font for Windows Terminal
The new Cascadia Code Font for Windows Terminal
The new Cascadia Code Font for Windows Terminal
The new Cascadia Code Font for Windows Terminal
The new Cascadia Code Font for Windows Terminal
The new Cascadia Code Font for Windows Terminal
```

Figure 1.5 – The Cascadia Code font at a selection of font weights

Cascadia Code currently has support for a wide range of characters, including Cyrillic, Greek, and Vietnamese. It's open source, licensed under the SIL Open Font License, so progress for supporting additional languages can be tracked on GitHub, at `https://github.com/microsoft/cascadia-code/`.

Cascadia Code is called a programming font due to its support for optional programming ligatures. A ligature is a font feature that allows multiple characters to be rendered as a single glyph. For example, when typing the characters in the first row in the following image, they will be rendered as the bottom row:

$$=> \quad >= \quad <= \quad != $$
$$\Rightarrow \quad \geq \quad \leq \quad \neq$$

Figure 1.6 – Top: characters as typed and stored. Bottom: ligatures as rendered

In addition to programming ligatures, Cascadia Code also supports Powerline glyphs, a popular terminal customization that can improve the look of the command-line prompt, making it stand out from the input/output text around it:

Figure 1.7 – Powerline prompt rendered using Cascadia Code PL

As mentioned, all these features are optional—the Cascadia font comes in four variations that allow enabling or disabling of both programming ligatures and Powerline glyphs:

	Powerline Disabled	Powerline Enabled
Ligature Support Disabled	Cascadia Mono	Cascadia Mono PL
Ligature Support Enabled	Cascadia Code	Cascadia Code PL

Figure 1.8 – Cascadia font variations

We'll cover Powerline customization in detail in *Chapter 5, Changing your Windows Terminal appearance.*

Flexible JSON-based customization

Customization of the old terminal was quite frustrating; the options were distributed across both the Windows Registry and inside the shortcut files themselves! The new Windows Terminal fixes this and features a `settings.json` file with a documented schema.

The benefit of using a JSON file with a schema is two-fold: editors such as Visual Studio Code can provide a first-class editing experience with documentation and autocomplete, and the `settings.json` file can be version-controlled and easily shared across computers.

Figure 1.9 – Editing settings.json in Visual Studio Code, with autocompletion of available settings

Additionally, the built-in **Settings UI** provides an easier way to customize the terminal. The Settings UI still uses the settings.json file behind the scenes, so the resulting configuration can still be easily shared and version controlled.

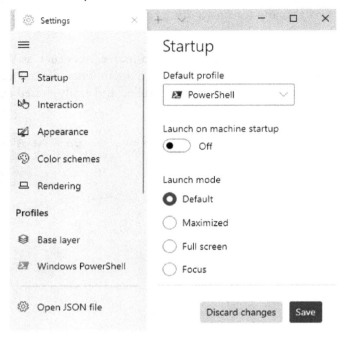

Figure 1.10 – The Settings UI in Windows Terminal

The settings.json file controls all aspects of the terminal, such as its themes and colors, keybindings, and window behavior. We'll dive deep into this file in *Chapter 4, Customizing your Windows Terminal settings*.

Open source development

The new Windows Terminal is open source! All development happens on Microsoft's GitHub repository, at https://github.com/microsoft/terminal/. The development team is incredibly active in this repository; bug reports, feature planning, and feature development happens in the open. Reading through this code repository, downloading the code, and even contributing to it is encouraged!

Figure 1.11 – The Windows Terminal GitHub repository

In addition to open source code, the documentation itself is open source. The documentation is hosted at `https://aka.ms/terminal-docs`, and clicking the **Edit this Document** link will navigate to the relevant document on GitHub. Edits to the documentation follow the typical pull request process, using Markdown for formatting.

The repository has hundreds of open source contributors, working on all aspects of the terminal. Several major features, such as background image support, have been added by the community. Whether it's improving documentation, submitting bug reports, or discussing and then adding features, feel free to get involved! Check out the `CONTRIBUTING.md` file in the GitHub repository to get started.

Now that we've covered the benefits of the new Windows Terminal, let's take our first step and get it installed!

Installing Windows Terminal

There are several ways to get the new Windows Terminal. The easiest and recommended way is to install it from the Microsoft Store. The Microsoft Store is part of Windows 10 and will ensure we have a seamless installation experience. Updates to Windows Terminal are also delivered through the Microsoft Store.

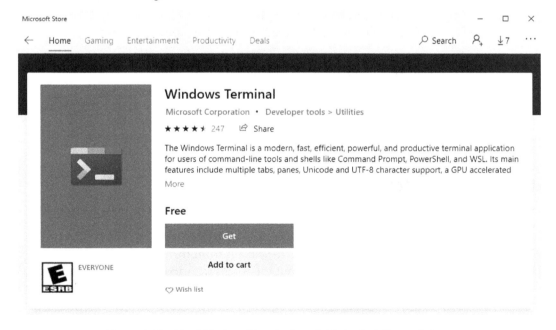

Figure 1.12 – The Windows Terminal available in the Microsoft Store

1. From the Windows Start menu, search for the `Microsoft Store` and open it.

2. From inside the Microsoft Store, search for `Windows Terminal`.

3. Select **Windows Terminal** and then click **Get**.

4. Wait for Windows Terminal to download and install.

5. Optionally, inside the Microsoft Store app, enable automatic updates by going to **Settings** and select **Update apps automatically**.

While this is the best way to both install the new Windows Terminal and ensure it stays up to date, there are several other ways to install Windows Terminal that might better fit certain automation scenarios:

- Using the command-line `winget` installer:

```
winget install --id=Microsoft.WindowsTerminal -e
```

- Using the command-line chocolatey installer (unofficial):

```
choco install microsoft-windows-terminal
```

- Advanced users can download a pre-built release from GitHub, located at `https://github.com/microsoft/terminal/releases`. Install the Desktop Bridge VC++ v14 Redistributable Package as a dependency first.

- Advanced users may also be interested in the *Windows Terminal Preview* application from the Microsoft Store, which can be installed alongside the Windows Terminal application. Windows Terminal Preview provides access to the latest features, though there may be some stability issues.

Now that we have Windows Terminal installed, let's start it up!

Launching Windows Terminal

It's worth spending some time reviewing how to efficiently start our Windows Terminal, as it's something we'll be doing frequently!

The normal way to start Windows Terminal is to select it from the Start menu, either by selecting the icon using the mouse or typing out the words `windows terminal` in the Start menu search bar.

Luckily, there are faster ways. Windows Terminal ships with a binary, wt.exe, that can be used to quickly start the terminal. Press *wt<enter>* from the Start menu, Run dialog, or Windows Explorer location bar to open the terminal. wt.exe has several interesting command-line flags, such as -F to launch in fullscreen mode. We'll learn more about the capabilities of wt.exe in *Chapter 6, Setting up keyboard shortcuts*.

An additional way to start Windows Terminal is to use the taskbar keyboard shortcuts, such as *Win + 1*, *Win + 2*, and so on. Pin the application to the taskbar by finding the Windows Terminal application in the Start menu, right-clicking it, and choosing **Pin to taskbar**. Then, on the taskbar, drag the Windows Terminal icon all the way to the left so it's the leftmost icon. Now, pressing *Win + 1* will launch Windows Terminal, or bring it into the foreground if it's already open:

Figure 1.13 –Windows Terminal pinned to the taskbar in the first position

Now that we have the Windows Terminal pinned to the taskbar, we can right-click on the icon to open a *Jump List Menu*, where we can open Windows Terminal directly to our desired shell:

Figure 1.14 – The Windows 10 Jump List for the Windows Terminal

The final way we'll learn to open Windows Terminal is from Windows Explorer. Open Windows Explorer (*Win* + *E*) and then right-click any directory. Select the **Open in Windows Terminal** menu item to open that directory in Windows Terminal. Additionally, right-clicking or pressing *Shift* and right-clicking on the background of Windows Explorer shows an **Open Windows Terminal here** menu option that will open the current directory in Windows Terminal:

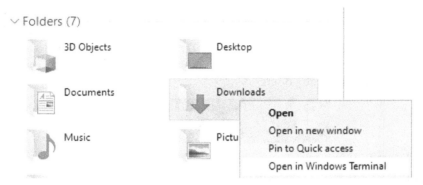

Figure 1.15 – The Open in Windows Terminal context menu item

Summary

In this chapter, we learned the differences between a terminal and a shell. We discussed how the new Windows Terminal has several key benefits over the older `conhost.exe`, including a modern, GPU-accelerated UI, a flexible JSON-based configuration system, and an open source community. In addition, we learned a few ways of installing the new Windows Terminal, as well as how to efficiently launch it from anywhere in Windows 10.

In the next chapter, we'll learn how to effectively use Windows Terminal. We'll cover all major components of Windows Terminal, including the terminal tabs, panes, and interacting with various shells. We'll also cover a few interesting keyboard shortcuts, as well as the new command palette feature.

Further reading

If you found the discussion of terminals versus shells interesting, you may also enjoy reading about ConPTY—the new modern console infrastructure that enabled Windows Terminal to be possible in the first place! Rich Turner, when he was the Senior Program Manager of Windows Console and Command Line, wrote an excellent blog post series titled *Windows Command-Line* that walks through the nitty-gritty details: `https://devblogs.microsoft.com/commandline/windows-command-line-backgrounder/`.

If you're interested in learning more about the modern technology powering the new Windows Terminal, check out *Building Windows Terminal with WinUI* by Kayla Cinnamon, the Program Manager of Windows Terminal, Console, Command Line, and Cascadia Code: `https://devblogs.microsoft.com/commandline/building-windows-terminal-with-winui/`.

2
Learning the Windows Terminal UI

Windows Terminal has a rich **user interface** (**UI**) for managing shells, including PowerShell and the command prompt, and supports both mouse usage and keyboard shortcuts. In this chapter, we'll take a look at the capabilities of the Windows Terminal UI and learn how to use it efficiently.

As Windows Terminal is primarily about the command line and keyboard, it supports an extensive and flexible keyboard shortcut system. When discussing keyboard shortcuts in this chapter, we will cover the default keyboard shortcuts available and the rationale for choosing these keys. However, these keyboard shortcuts are configurable and can be rebound to different keys, a topic we'll cover in *Chapter 6, Setting up keyboard shortcuts*.

By the end of this chapter, we will be proficient with the entire Windows Terminal UI and the majority of the keyboard shortcuts. We'll explore the following topics:

- Using the terminal tabs
- Using terminal panes
- Managing terminal output

- Using the command palette
- Keyboard shortcuts review

Once we complete these topics, we'll have the solid foundation required for delving into more advanced areas of Windows Terminal.

Technical requirements

The only requirement started is to have the new Windows Terminal installed! Refer to the previous chapter's *Installing Windows Terminal* section if you don't already have it.

Using the terminal tabs

One of the headline features of Windows Terminal is the tab UI, which helps when performing multiple tasks simultaneously. In the old Windows terminal, `conhost.exe`, the main way of performing multiple tasks was to have multiple windows open at the same time. However, this can result in "losing" the terminal windows amidst all the other applications that are open, and it can be frustrating to find the correct terminal when *Alt +* tabbing between applications.

Additionally, Windows 10, like other operating systems, supports multiple different shells. Out of the box, Windows includes PowerShell and the command prompt, with additional shells such as PowerShell Core and those under Windows Subsystem for Linux just a few clicks away. With the older `conhost.exe`, each of these shells would typically each have their own window, further increasing our multiple window woes:

Figure 2.1 – Quick! Which window is that terminal we were looking for again?

While Windows Terminal supports multiple windows, just like PowerShell and the command prompt, it also supports terminal tabs. These tabs can be controlled with two different buttons, a **plus button** and a **downward arrow button**:

Figure 2.2 – An open tab, with the plus button and downward arrow button for managing shells

Clicking the plus button, or pressing the *Ctrl + Shift + T* keyboard shortcut, will immediately open a new tab with our default shell. To close the tab, press the × button in the tab header or press the *Ctrl + Shift + W* shortcut. These keyboard shortcuts should hopefully be unsurprising; they mirror the *de facto* standard shortcuts for managing browser tabs (*Ctrl + T* and *Ctrl + W*).

Clicking the downward arrow button, or pressing *Ctrl + Shift + Space*, will open the **new shell dropdown menu**. Windows Terminal will dynamically populate this menu with the shells installed on our system, assigning a keyboard shortcut for each. We can see an example of this in *Figure 2.3*.

On some locales, this keyboard shortcut conflicts with the Windows 10 keyboard shortcut for switching input methods, such as between Chinese (Simplified) and Chinese (Traditional). If *Ctrl + Shift + Space* isn't working, we'll see how to rebind these keys in *Chapter 6*, *Setting up keyboard shortcuts*:

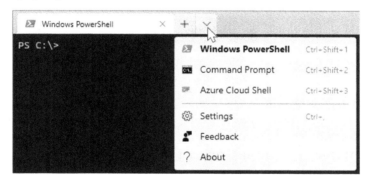

Figure 2.3 – The new shell dropdown menu. Depending on your system, you may have
a different list of shells

In *Figure 2.3*, Windows Terminal has auto-discovered PowerShell, the command prompt, and Azure Cloud Shell on our system, and placed them into the drop-down menu. Pressing *Ctrl + Shift + 1* will open a PowerShell tab, and pressing *Ctrl + Shift + 2* will open a command prompt. *Ctrl + Shift + D* will open a "duplicate" of the currently active tab. In *Figure 2.3*, since the active tab is PowerShell, *Ctrl + Shift + D* will open a new PowerShell tab.

> **Note**
> As of Windows Terminal 1.6, the duplicated tab does not automatically use the same working directory as the original tab. We'll see how to enable this behavior for PowerShell tabs in *Chapter 8, Tips for using PowerShell like a Pro*.

To switch between tabs, in addition to clicking a tab with the mouse, pressing *Ctrl + Tab* will navigate to the next tab, and *Ctrl + Shift + Tab* will navigate back. To navigate to a specific tab, press *Ctrl + Alt + [1-9]* to activate the tab at that index. Tabs also support drag-and-drop reordering.

Editing tab title appearance

Windows Terminal supports editing both the color of a tab and its title text, in order to differentiate one tab from all the others. This can be useful, for example, when connecting remotely to a critical system.

Let's use both these features together and make a tab entitled "**Production**" and colored bright red. Right-click on a tab and select **Color...** to open a color picker. After selecting the red color, click the **Rename Tab** option to open an editor inside the tab bar. Set the name to "Production" and press *Enter*. We'll end up with something like *Figure 2.4*. The tab color is temporary; if we close the tab, the changes aren't remembered:

Figure 2.4 – The "Production" tab is colored red. If you purchased a physical book (thanks!), you get to enjoy it in grayscale

Windows Terminal has some other ways of managing tabs that are, by default, not available in the UI or via keyboard shortcuts. We'll learn about these useful commands in *Chapter 7, Hidden Windows Terminal Actions*. For now, let's move on to another useful, built-in feature of Windows Terminal: terminal panes!

Using terminal panes

Tabs are just one way of managing multiple tasks; the other way is to use terminal panes. Panes are a way of opening side-by-side shells within the same tab. They're useful when working with the output of multiple commands at the same time. For example, one pane can execute a long-running `tracert` command, while the other is left free for executing more exploratory commands:

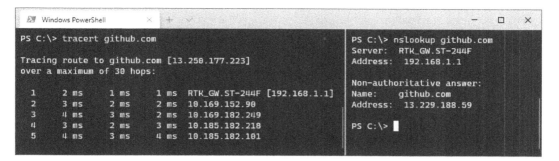

Figure 2.5 – Windows Terminal with two panes. Left: a pane running a lengthy tracert command.
Right: a pane we can use while waiting for the tracert command to complete

The same **plus** and **downward arrow** buttons we used to create tabs can also be used to create panes. Just hold down the *Alt* key while clicking the buttons:

- Holding *Alt* while clicking the plus button will open the default shell in a new pane.

- Holding *Alt* while selecting a shell from the **new shell dropdown menu** will open that shell in a new pane.

Like tabs, panes support a rich set of keyboard shortcuts. The primary shortcut for opening a new pane is *Alt + Shift + D*, which will duplicate the current shell into a new pane. Note the similarity to the *Ctrl + Shift + D* shortcut (duplicate new tab) discussed in the previous section; this demonstrates how panes and tabs use similar shortcuts, differing only by the *Alt* versus *Ctrl* modifiers, respectively. This is a useful mnemonic that will help with the fast and natural use of the keyboard.

When creating a pane with the *Alt + Shift + D* shortcut or the buttons on the UI, Windows Terminal will try to "do the right thing" and open a horizontal or vertical pane, whichever one leads to the most square shape. To control the layout exactly, use the *Alt + Shift + Minus* key to open a new default shell horizontally. This keyboard shortcut can be remembered because the shape of the horizontal pane corresponds to the horizontal line of the minus character. The neighboring key, *Alt + Shift + Equals*, will open a new pane vertically. Again, the vertical shape of the pane corresponds to the vertically stacked lines of the equals character.

To switch between active panes, pressing *Alt + Arrow* (the *Up, Down, Left*, or *Right* arrows) will switch to the pane in the direction of the arrow key, and any pane can be clicked with the mouse to activate it. Resizing the panes follows a similar pattern: *Alt + Shift + Arrow* will resize the active pane in that direction:

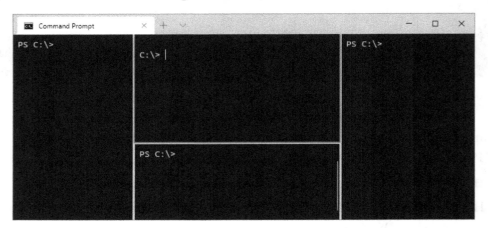

Figure 2.6 – Creating flexible terminal layouts with the Alt + Shift + minus, Alt + Shift + equals, and Alt + Shift + arrow keys

Finally, we can close a pane by pressing *Ctrl + Shift + W*. Attentive readers will notice that this keyboard shortcut does not follow the "Alt key" pattern covered earlier for managing panes. This is the same keyboard shortcut we use to close tabs. This one shortcut can close anything (pane or tab) in Windows Terminal.

Now that we know how to use Windows Terminal's tabs and panes to manage "around" our shells, let's look at managing the output inside them!

Managing terminal output

When using the terminal, the amount of output from commands typically outweighs the amount of input; it's easy to get overwhelmed! Let's look at some tools built into Windows Terminal that help us to manage terminal output.

The most typical way of managing output is with shell-specific commands; for example, you may use `findstr` in the command prompt, `Select-String` in PowerShell, or `grep` on Linux/Unix shells. However, Windows Terminal also includes its own tools that work on output from any shell. Since Windows Terminal is handling the output of these shells, it can also provide unified tooling.

To search the output of any shell, press *Ctrl + Shift + F* to open the search bar:

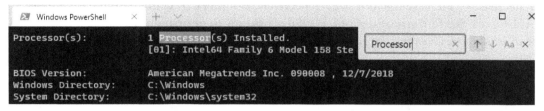

Figure 2.7 – Searching the output of the "systeminfo" command

Typing any search term and pressing *Enter* will find that term in the currently active pane or tab, starting from the bottom and going up. Subsequent presses of *Enter* will find subsequent occurrences of the search term, and *Shift + Enter* will reverse the search direction. Pressing the Aa icon will toggle case-sensitive searching.

Another common task with terminals is copying output onto the clipboard. This task has a surprising nuance: *Ctrl + C* is the most natural keyboard shortcut for copying text, but *Ctrl + C* has historically also been used to interrupt long-running commands. Windows Terminal therefore has the following behavior for copying text:

- *Ctrl + Shift + C* will always copy selected text. If there's no text selected, then nothing happens.

- *Ctrl + C* will copy text if text is selected; otherwise *Ctrl + C* will interrupt the currently running command.

- Right-clicking when text is selected will copy that text.

- Windows Terminal also supports **copy on select** mode, in which selecting text with the mouse will automatically copy it to the clipboard. This functionality is disabled by default; we'll cover how to enable it in *Chapter 4, Customizing your Windows Terminal settings*.

Thankfully, pasting is much more straightforward. The typical *Ctrl + V* keyboard shortcut will paste, as expected, as well as *Ctrl + Shift + V* and *Shift + insert*; these latter keyboard shortcuts are useful when a command-line application is overriding *Ctrl + V*. Additionally, Windows Terminal supports **mouse-based pasting**; clicking the right mouse button will paste from the clipboard if no text is selected. Mouse-based pasting, when combined with the copy on select functionality mentioned above, can lead to very fast and fluid copy/paste operations.

Finally, if the terminal output is too big or too small, pressing *Ctrl + Minus* or *Ctrl + Plus* will decrease or increase the font size, respectively. Holding *Ctrl* while scrolling the mouse will also scale the font size as desired. We'll discuss how to permanently change the font size in *Chapter 4, Customizing your Windows Terminal settings*, as well:

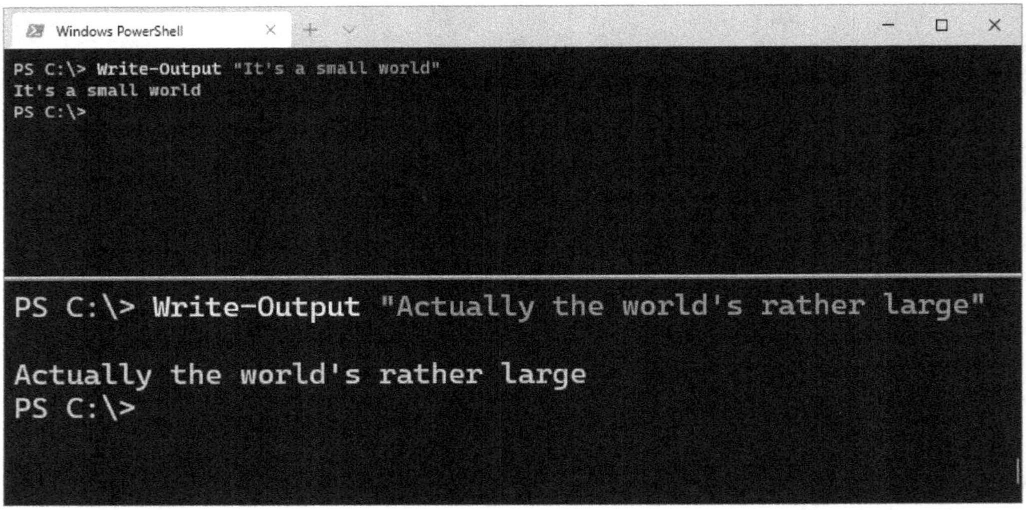

Figure 2.8 – Zoom levels in Windows Terminal are supported per pane

Now, we've covered a lot of keyboard shortcuts in these past few sections, and it can be daunting to remember them all! Luckily, the final Windows Terminal feature we'll be discussing is built to help: the **command palette**.

Using the command palette

The **command palette**, initially popularized by Visual Studio Code, also makes an appearance in Windows Terminal. It even uses the same keyboard shortcut as Visual Studio Code, *Ctrl + Shift + P*, so the muscle memory is transferable.

The command palette is a great way to discover commands in Windows Terminal. For example, pretend we forget how to duplicate a pane. We probably don't even remember the "duplicate" word; we just know we want to do something with a pane! Pressing *Ctrl + Shift + P* will open the command palette, and then typing the word pane will return all pane-related commands, including our forgotten **Duplicate pane** command:

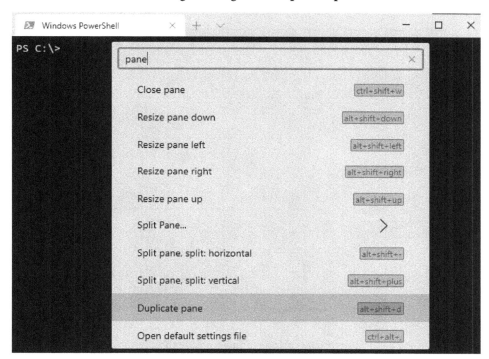

Figure 2.9 – Using the command palette to find the "Duplicate pane" command

The best part about the command palette is that it shows the associated keyboard shortcuts for each command (*Alt + Shift + D* in our "Duplicate pane" example). It functions not only as a fast command access tool, but also as a teaching tool that will help remind us of the shortcuts for the future.

The command palette additionally supports multiple-level menus. For example, if we search for split pane, we'll see the ">" icon, indicating that a submenu is available. These submenus will guide us through the various options we have when opening a new pane. First, we'll select **Split Pane...**, then we'll select a shell, and finally we'll choose the pane direction (auto, horizontal, or vertical). We can navigate back and forth through these submenus using the < and > icons, respectively:

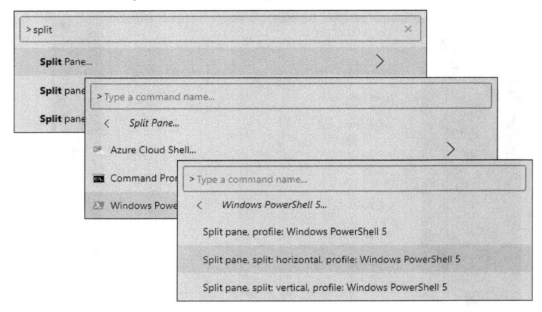

Figure 2.10 – A multi-level menu guiding us through splitting a pane

If you only remember one keyboard shortcut from this chapter, make sure it's *Ctrl + Shift + P*! This shortcut will act as a gateway to all the other keyboard shortcuts. As Windows Terminal inevitably adds additional keyboard shortcuts and features in the future, the command palette will list them in a convenient, searchable list.

Keyboard shortcuts review

We've covered a lot of keyboard shortcuts throughout this chapter. Let's do a quick review and make sure they feel natural:

- Tabs:

    a) *Ctrl + Shift + T* – Opens a new tab

    b) *Ctrl + Shift + Space* – Opens the new shell drop-down menu

c) *Ctrl + Shift + [1-9]* – Opens a new tab with the shell specified by the number (as listed in the new shell drop-down menu)

d) *Ctrl + Shift + D* – Duplicates the currently active shell into a new tab

e) *Ctrl + Tab / Ctrl + Shift + Tab* – Activates the next/previous tab

f) *Ctrl + Alt + [1-9]* – Activates the tab at the index specified by the number

g) *Ctrl + Shift + W* – Closes the current tab or pane

- Panes:

a) *Alt* + click on the new tab button – Opens a new pane with the default shell

b) *Alt* + click on a shell in the new shell drop-down menu – Opens a new pane with the selected shell

c) *Alt + Shift + D* – Duplicates the currently active shell into a new pane

d) *Alt + Shift + Minus* – Opens a new default shell horizontally

e) *Alt + Shift + Equals* – Opens a new default shell vertically

f) *Alt + Arrow* – Activates the pane in the direction of the arrow

g) *Alt + Shift + Arrow* – Resizes the active pane in the direction of the arrow

h) *Ctrl + Shift + W* – Closes the current tab or pane

- Searching:

a) *Ctrl + Shift + F* – Opens the search bar

b) *Enter* – Finds the next match, searching up

c) *Shift + Enter* – Finds the previous match, searching down

- General:

a) *Ctrl + Shift + C* – Copies selected text

b) *Ctrl + C* – Copies text if selected, otherwise, it cancels the current command

c) *Ctrl + V* – Pastes

d) *Ctrl + Plus / Ctrl + Minus* – Zooms in/out

e) *Ctrl + Shift + P* – Opens the command palette

If a particular keyboard shortcut feels weird, unnatural or even missing—don't worry! We'll cover how to rebind keys and create our own custom bound commands in *Chapter 6, Setting up keyboard shortcuts.*

Summary

We've now covered all the major parts of Windows Terminal, including terminal tabs, panes, keyboard shortcuts, the search UI, and the command palette. We now have the solid foundation we need to be command line masters—and it's only *Chapter 2*!

The remainder of this book will focus on customizing our Windows Terminal and its shells to bring our command-line usage to the next level. We'll cover installing additional shells, advanced customization techniques, and example development and DevOps workflows for building and deploying real-world applications.

Let's jump into our first advanced topic in the book: adding a fully functioning Ubuntu Linux environment into Windows, easily accessible through our new shell drop-down menu in Windows Terminal.

Further reading

To stay up to date on the newest features of the Windows Terminal UI, check out the Windows Terminal overview at `https://docs.microsoft.com/en-us/windows/terminal/`. It features animated GIFs of many of the features we've covered in this chapter.

3
Configuring an Ubuntu Linux profile

Earlier, we discussed how Windows Terminal excels at discovering and managing different shells on our system. Up until this point, however, we've only seen the PowerShell and Command Prompt shells in action. As our first alternative shell of the book, let's install and use Bash on Ubuntu, from inside Windows Terminal! In this chapter, we'll install the **Windows Subsystem for Linux, version 2 (WSL2)** and learn how to use it from inside our terminal.

By the end of this chapter, we will have an Ubuntu shell installed on our system, and will be able to launch it from Windows Terminal. We'll cover the following topics:

- Why use the Windows Subsystem for Linux?
- Installing Ubuntu Linux
- Installing Linux applications: nginx
- Bidirectional access in Windows and Ubuntu

Readers with WSL2 already installed may wish to start reading the *Installing Linux Applications: nginx* section. Additionally, we'll cover some advanced configurations in *Chapter 9, Tips for using Ubuntu like an Expert*.

Technical requirements

To install WSL2, you'll need to have an up-to-date Windows installation running at least the May 2019 update (version 1903, as reported in the output of the winver command). If you're running an ARM64 system, you'll need version 2004.

Additionally, your computer will need to support hardware virtualization. Most computers do, but it may not be enabled in the BIOS. If you run into virtualization problems, check your PC's manufacturer for information on how to enable hardware virtualization. We'll be modifying some configuration files in this chapter. All code and configuration from this chapter can be found at `https://github.com/PacktPublishing/Windows-Terminal-Tips-Tricks/tree/main/Chapter 03`.

Why use the Windows Subsystem for Linux?

Sometimes, certain tasks, such as frontend development or server management, are easier on Linux/Unix systems. While most popular frameworks, tools, and programming languages support both Windows and Linux, it's common to find parts of the ecosystem that don't; common culprits are smaller third-party libraries, plugins, or packages.

WSL2 provides a fast, lightweight way to run Linux programs on Windows. In this way, it's similar to Cygwin or MinGW. WSL2 has several benefits over these existing tools; it's faster, more compatible, and has deep integration with Windows 10. Many popular Linux distributions, such as Ubuntu, SUSE, Kali, and more, are available directly from the Microsoft Store, and Linux kernel updates are provided through Windows Update.

> **Note: WSL1 versus WSL2**
>
> The Windows Subsystem for Linux has two different versions. Version 1, initially released in 2016, was essentially a translation layer between Linux and Windows system calls. While this worked reasonably well, there were some shortcomings regarding speed and software compatibility.
>
> In May 2019, Microsoft announced the radically rearchitected Windows Subsystem for Linux 2, which was released in May 2020. This version ran a real Linux kernel on Hyper-V virtualization, rather than using a system call translation layer. It resulted in a 3 to 5 times faster experience, sometimes reaching up to 20 times faster for certain workloads.
>
> Interested in learning more? Documentation is available at `https://docs.microsoft.com/en-us/windows/wsl/about`. For advanced architectural information, watch the video *The new Windows subsystem for Linux architecture: a deep dive – BRK3068*, at `https://youtu.be/lwhMThePdIo`.

WSL2 is primarily targeted at running command-line applications, such as the GNU coreutils (cat, ls, grep, and so on) or server applications such as Redis and nginx. While work is underway for graphical programs, where WSL2 really shines is at the command line. Additionally, WSL2 is not intended for production hosting; it's focused on running development and DevOps tasks on the local computer. Let's see this in action by installing Ubuntu—on Windows!

Installing Ubuntu Linux

Installing Ubuntu on WSL2 has two main steps. First, we'll enable the WSL2 system on our computer. Second, we'll choose the Ubuntu distribution to install in WSL2. While we will cover the basic steps here, the most up-to-date instructions and troubleshooting information can always be found at `https://docs.microsoft.com/en-us/windows/wsl/install-win10`.

Microsoft is currently working on streamlining the first step by adding a `wsl --install` command, which can be run from Windows Terminal with administrator privileges. Until that's ready, though, we'll need to manually install WSL2 by following *Step 1*.

Step 1: Install WSL2

First, we'll enable the required Windows 10 features. From the start menu, search for **Turn Windows Features on or off** and then enable two features, the **Virtual Machine Platform** and the **Windows Subsystem for Linux**:

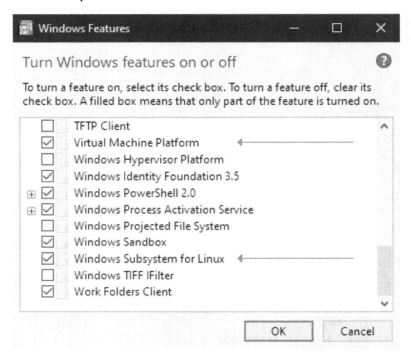

Figure 3.1 – Adding the two Windows features required for WSL2

Once the installation is complete, reboot the computer. Next, open Windows Terminal as an administrator, and execute the following command to set WSL2 as the default for new Linux installations:

```
wsl --set-default-version 2
```

If onscreen instructions are displayed in the output, follow these instructions before continuing to *Step 2*.

Step 2: Install Ubuntu

Open the Microsoft Store and search for Linux. Pause for a moment and contemplate how incredible that previous sentence is!

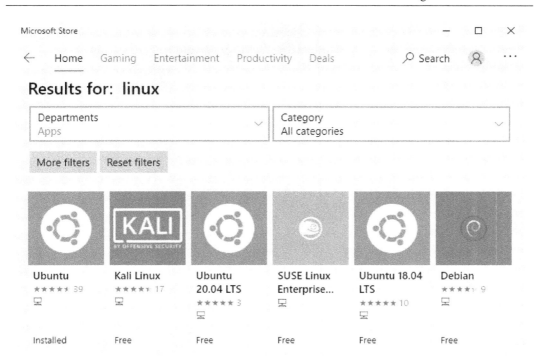

Figure 3.2 – Linux distributions inside the Microsoft Store

Choose a Linux distribution. In this chapter, we'll be selecting and installing Ubuntu. Don't worry too much about which one to choose—WSL2 supports running different distributions side by side. Click **Get** and wait for the installation to complete.

Launching Linux

Once the installation is complete, launch Linux from the start menu by searching for the name of the distribution. In our case, we'll search for Ubuntu and run it.

It will take a minute to do some first-time setup, eventually prompting for a new username:

```
Ubuntu                                                    —   □   ×
Please create a default UNIX user account. The username does not need to ma
tch your Windows username.
For more information visit: https://aka.ms/wslusers
Enter new UNIX username: _
```

Figure 3.3 – Ubuntu's first-time setup prompting for a new UNIX username

Once account creation is complete, close the window and start up Windows Terminal. Windows Terminal will detect the Ubuntu installation and automatically add it to the list of available shells:

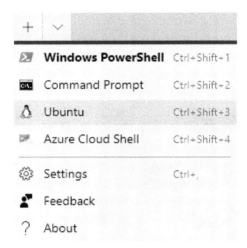

Figure 3.4 – Ubuntu, autodiscovered by Windows Terminal

Currently, our icon for Ubuntu is a general "tux" icon that represents Linux. We'll cover how to change this icon in *Chapter 4, Customizing your Windows Terminal settings*.

Click on **Ubuntu**, and Ubuntu Linux will open up in a new tab. Additionally, holding *Alt* while clicking **Ubuntu** will open it up in a new pane, so we can literally run PowerShell side by side with Ubuntu. Next, let's see what we can do with it.

Installing Linux applications: nginx

We've just installed a fully functioning Ubuntu operating system inside Windows 10. Let's familiarize ourselves with it by performing a task we might need to perform in the real world. We'll install and configure **nginx**, the most popular web server software in the world. Nginx powers about 30% of the entire web, and is a very common deploy target for web-based software.

We'll install nginx using **apt**, the built-in package manager for Ubuntu. First, we'll update our list of available packages:

```
sudo apt update
```

Next, we'll install nginx:

```
sudo apt install nginx
```

With just two commands, we've now installed nginx. These steps are the same steps we'd take if we were running Ubuntu natively installed on our computer or server. The binaries we're downloading and installing as part of the `apt install` command are *not* special versions for Windows; they're native binaries and scripts directly from Ubuntu's repositories.

Starting nginx

When starting a web server such as nginx, it will, by default, try to listen on port 80. If IIS is already running on that port, nginx will be unable to start listening. To be safe, let's change nginx to listen on port 8000 to avoid this conflict:

1. Open the nginx configuration file using the nano editor. Vim is also available:

    ```
    sudo nano /etc/nginx/sites-enabled/default
    ```

2. Scroll down a bit, and change the line that reads `listen 80 default_server;` to `listen 8000 default_server;`:

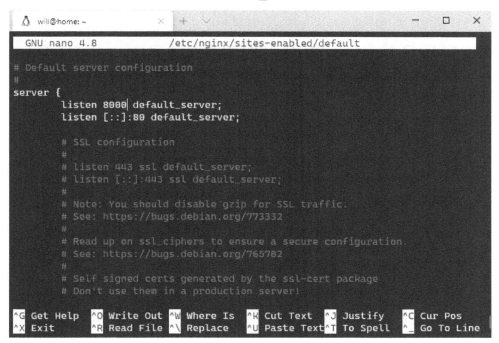

Figure 3.5 – Changing the default nginx port by editing the configuration file in nano

3. After saving the file (*Ctrl* + *O*) and exiting the configuration file (*Ctrl* + *X*), start the nginx service by running `sudo service nginx start`.

4. Finally, in a web browser, navigate to `http://localhost:8000` and enjoy the nginx welcome page! This means that nginx is successfully running in Ubuntu, and can be accessed from Windows. The networking setup is all handled transparently by WSL2:

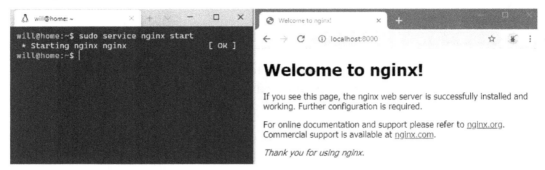

Figure 3.6 – Left: Starting the nginx service in Ubuntu. Right: Accessing nginx from Windows

Now that we've successfully installed and run an application in Linux, let's talk about files, and how to access Windows from Ubuntu, and Ubuntu from Windows.

Bidirectional access in Windows and Ubuntu

With Windows and Ubuntu side by side, let's explore how to access one from the other. First, we'll look at our filesystem with `ls`:

```
$ ls /
bin    etc    lib    libx32      mnt    root   snap   tmp
boot   home   lib32  lost+found  opt    run    srv    usr
dev    init   lib64  media              proc   sbin   sys    var
```

Figure 3.7 – Filesystem with ls command

This is a normal Ubuntu Linux filesystem. If we look inside the `mnt` directory, we'll find a `c` directory. Inside this `c` directory is our Windows installation. From Ubuntu's perspective, our Windows hard drive is "mounted" inside Linux:

```
$ ls /mnt/c
'$Recycle.Bin'              'System Volume Information'
'$WINDOWS.~BT'              Temp
 Backups                    Users
'Documents and Settings'    Windows
 Microsoft                  hiberfil.sys
 PerfLogs                   inetpub
'Program Files'             pagefile.sys
'Program Files (x86)'       swapfile.sys
```

Figure 3.8 – The Windows C: drive is mounted under /mnt/c

If we wish to go the other way around, and view our Ubuntu files from Windows, we can simply run Windows Explorer from inside WSL2 by typing `explorer.exe .` (that is, the Windows Explorer executable with the current directory, .):

Figure 3.9 – Accessing Ubuntu's filesystem from Windows

When Windows Explorer opens, it shows the path `\\wsl$\Ubuntu` in the address bar. If we had another distribution installed, such as Debian, the path would be `\\wsl$\Debian`. This style of path, known as a **universal naming convention path** (UNC path), is used frequently in Windows to refer to network resources. Our WSL2 installation is entirely local, but it's convenient to use UNC paths as they're widely compatible with other Windows applications.

Attentive readers will notice that we just ran `explorer.exe`, a decidedly Windows command, from inside Ubuntu. Any Windows executable can run from inside Ubuntu, as long as it's suffixed with `.exe`. For example, `ping example.com` will run the Linux ping command, and `ping.exe example.com` will run the Windows ping command. We could even run `powershell.exe` from inside WSL2! PowerShell would see the current Linux directory represented as a UNC path.

We've now covered the basics of WSL2—we have a fully functioning Linux command line available from inside our Windows Terminal. We'll come back to WSL2 in later chapters and learn even more productivity tips!

Summary

In this chapter, we learned that by using WSL2, we double the universe of software that is available to us. We installed WSL2 and then Ubuntu, and saw how Windows Terminal autodiscovers Ubuntu and provides easy tab and pane access to it.

In addition, we installed nginx using the apt package manager, and saw how WSL2 provides transparent network access to allow us to easily access nginx from Windows. We also learned how WSL2 and Windows integrate to provide easy file access between both systems.

Next up, let's dive into the various customization options that Windows Terminal provides through its flexible `settings.json` system.

Section 2: Configuring your Windows Terminal and its shells

In the previous section, we learned how to use Windows Terminal; in this section, we'll dive deep into its customization and advanced use. We'll learn how to customize both behavior and appearance to create highly optimized and beautiful terminal environments, and cover tips and tricks for getting the most out of Windows Terminal, PowerShell, and WSL2.

This section comprises the following chapters:

- *Chapter 4, Customizing your Windows Terminal settings*
- *Chapter 5, Changing your Windows Terminal appearance*
- *Chapter 6, Setting up keyboard shortcuts*
- *Chapter 7, Hidden Windows Terminal Actions*
- *Chapter 8, Tips for using PowerShell like a Pro*
- *Chapter 9, Tips for using Ubuntu like an Expert*

4
Customizing your Windows Terminal settings

One of the cornerstones of Windows Terminal is its configurability: it exposes a wealth of settings, each with a sensible default. In this chapter, we'll cover how this configuration system works, and highlight some of the more interesting settings.

We'll also take our first look at Windows Terminal's **custom profile** feature, which supports running arbitrary commands as shells. We'll add a couple of useful custom profiles; for example, a profile that can open terminal tabs to remote systems.

By the end of the chapter, we will have covered both basic and advanced settings in Windows Terminal. We'll be discussing the following topics:

- Introducing the `settings.json` file
- The settings file structure
- Useful global settings
- Useful profile settings
- Custom command-line profiles

Technical requirements

We'll be modifying some configuration files in this chapter. All configuration files from this chapter can be found at `https://github.com/PacktPublishing/Windows-Terminal-Tips-Tricks/tree/main/Chapter 04`. This repository also contains a collection of nice icons for the custom profiles we'll be setting up in this chapter, so be sure to check them out!

Introducing the settings.json file

Windows Terminal uses a JSON file, named `settings.json`, for its underlying configuration store. This text-based format benefits the Windows Terminal development team by allowing them to rapidly iterate and release new settings. Additionally, it benefits users in that it can be stored in version control and easily synchronized across computers.

While there is ongoing work to create a UI for modifying these settings, as of 2021, the UI is undergoing rapid change, and does not currently support all the available settings. This book will generally refer to settings using the JSON keys and values, as they are unambiguous, less likely to change, and easier to copy/paste from the digital edition of the book. Additionally, a great deal of effort has gone into supporting a high-quality JSON editing experience. Let's test it out!

We can open the `settings.json` file by selecting the **Settings** menu item from the drop-down menu, and then selecting **Open JSON File**, or using the keyboard shortcut *Ctrl + Shift + ,*. The `settings.json` file will open in the default editor for the JSON file type. While any editor can be used to modify this file, **Visual Studio Code** will give the best experience by far; it is the editor we will be using for the remainder of the book. To change the default editor to Visual Studio Code, ensure it is installed and set it as the default editor for the `.json` file extension:

1. Create a new, empty file with the `.json` file extension on the Desktop.

2. Right-click the file and choose **Open with** and then **Choose another app**.

3. Select **Visual Studio Code**, ensure **Always use this app to open .json files** is checked, and then click **OK**. If Visual Studio Code is not available in the list of applications, expand the list, scroll down, and select **Look for another app on this PC**. Select `C:\Program Files\Microsoft VS Code\Code.exe`.

4. Delete the JSON file from *Step 1*.

One of the key features driving the JSON editing experience is the **JSON Schema** support. When an editor, such as Visual Studio Code, supports JSON Schema, we get autocompletion and integrated help documentation. Try using the mouse to hover over any setting to see the documentation; it will also display when editing a setting:

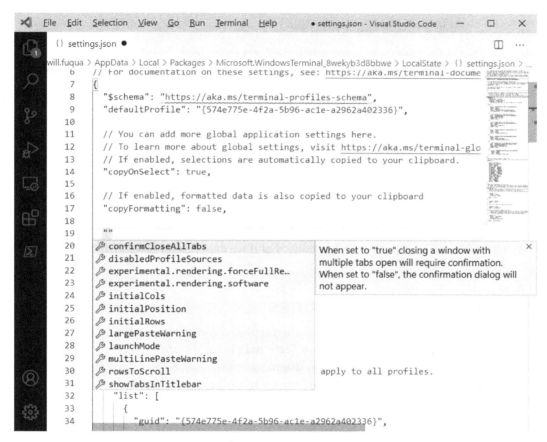

Figure 4.1 – Autocompletion and documentation in settings.json

Another key feature of the JSON editing experience is the **Apply on Save** functionality; after making a change to the settings, and saving the file, Windows Terminal will automatically apply the changes. If there's an error in the file, it will report the error, along with the line and column number of the invalid value:

Failed to reload settings

Settings could not be reloaded from file. Check for syntax errors, including trailing commas.
* Line 19, Column 26 (confirmCloseAllTabs)
  Have: "potato"
  Expected: true | false

Temporarily using the Windows Terminal default settings.

Figure 4.2 – An error message from an invalid settings.json file

Before we go much further, let's learn about how to recover from a bad setting. This way, we have the freedom to experiment, knowing that if we experiment too much, we can always get back to safety!

Recovering from bad settings

Editing a JSON file is not without its pitfalls; a misplaced comma or quote can completely invalidate the JSON file! Usually, Windows Terminal's error reporting, pictured earlier, is enough to solve the issue. However, if that doesn't work, we can back up and then delete the settings.json file entirely, and then relaunch Windows Terminal to generate a new, working settings.json file. The settings.json file is typically located in the C:\Users\{username}\AppData\Local\Packages\Microsoft. WindowsTerminal_8wekyb3d8bbwe\LocalState\ directory.

The settings file structure

While the autocomplete functionality goes a long way in helping us to explore available options, there is an alternate way. Windows Terminal uses two different settings files: the settings.json file, which we just opened, and the defaults.json file. This second file contains the settings with their default values in one, easy-to-read place. Windows Terminal will load the settings detailed in the defaults.json file first, and then layer the values from settings.json on top of the defaults.

This two-file approach allows the Windows Terminal team to ship new settings in the `defaults.json` file without disturbing the user's `settings.json` file. This means there's no point in editing the `defaults.json` file, as it's overwritten each time a new version of Windows Terminal is released. However, it's still useful to open it and get an overview of the available settings. Holding the *Alt* key while opening the **Settings** menu option, or pressing *Ctrl + Alt + Comma*, will open this `defaults.json` file.

We'll be spending the vast majority of our configuration efforts in the `settings.json` file. Let's get an overview of the major sections of this file:

1. Global settings

2. Profile settings

3. Color scheme settings

4. Keyboard shortcut settings

These four sections correspond with the following numbered areas in the `settings.json` file:

```
{
   // json schema to enable autocomplete and documentation
   "$schema": "https://aka.ms/terminal-profiles-schema",
   // 1. Global settings go at the top of the file.
   // 2. Profile settings go under the "profiles" key.
   "profiles":
   {
     "defaults":
     {
       // settings here apply to all profiles.
     },
     "list":
     [
       // per-profile settings
     ]
   },
   "schemes": [], // 3. Color scheme settings
   "actions":
   [
     // 4. Keyboard shortcut settings
   ]
}
```

In the remainder of this chapter, we'll cover the first two areas: global settings and profile settings. We'll cover the color scheme settings as part of *Chapter 5, Changing your Windows Terminal appearance*, and the keyboard shortcut settings in *Chapter 6, Setting up keyboard shortcuts*.

Useful Global Settings

Global settings control the parts of Windows Terminal that are common across all shells, like the tab UI and window settings. In this section, we'll explore some of the more interesting global settings:

- The `copyOnSelect` option, which defaults to `false`, will enable or disable automatically copying text to the clipboard immediately when the text is selected. Setting this to `true` works nicely with the **right-click to paste** functionality built into Windows Terminal.

- The `startOnUserLogin` option, which defaults to `false`, controls whether or not the terminal launches automatically when a user logs in to Windows 10.

- The `defaultProfile` option allows us to specify which shell is the default when we start Windows Terminal, or open a new pane or tab. We'll cover this setting in detail in the next section of this chapter.

- The `confirmCloseAllTabs` option, which defaults to `true`, will enable or disable the following dialog that shows when closing a window containing multiple tabs:

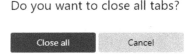

Figure 4.3 – The "Close all tabs?" dialog can be disabled via confirmCloseAllTabs

- The `showTabsInTitlebar` option, which defaults to `true`, controls whether the tabs render in Windows Terminal's titlebar, or in their own tabstrip beneath the titlebar. When both this option and the `alwaysShowTabs` option are set to `false`, and the terminal is restarted, Windows Terminal will hide the tab strip when only one tab is open. This results in a more traditional terminal that looks like the following:

Figure 4.4 – The terminal with only one tab open, and the tab strip hidden

Of course, this also hides the new tab buttons, so new tabs can be opened only via keyboard shortcuts such as *Ctrl + Shift + space* and *Ctrl + Shift + T*, or via the command palette (*Ctrl + Shift + P*).

- Finally, the theme option controls whether Windows Terminal uses a light theme or dark theme for the Windows Terminal UI widgets. It supports three values: light, dark, and system. The default is system, which follows the Windows 10 theming preference (**Turn on dark mode systemwide** from the start menu). We'll talk more about theming options in *Chapter 5*, *Changing your Windows Terminal appearance*.

That's all of the global settings we'll cover for the time being. Let's now move on to the next major configuration section – profile settings!

Useful profile settings

The profiles section of the settings.json file defines the shells that are available in the drop-down menu. For example, if Windows Terminal had three shells available in the menu, a possible configuration would look like this:

```
// ...
"profiles": {
  "defaults": { },
  "list": [
    {
      // Make changes here to the powershell profile.
      "guid": "{61c54bbd-c2c6-5271-96e7-009a87ff44bf}",
      "name": "Windows PowerShell 5",
      "commandline": "powershell.exe",
      "hidden": false
    },
    {
      "guid": "{0caa0dad-35be-5f56-a8ff-afceeeaa6101}",
```

```
      "name": "Command Prompt",
      "commandline": "cmd.exe",
      "hidden": false
    },
    {
      "guid": "{2c4de342-38b7-51cf-b940-2309a097f518}",
      "hidden": false,
      "name": "Ubuntu",
      "source": "Windows.Terminal.Wsl"
    }
  ]
}
// ...
```

Each profile object has a unique **GUID (globally unique identifier)**. This GUID can be referenced in the defaultProfile global setting to change the default shell launched on startup, as well as the shell launched when clicking the new tab button. However, this guid field is actually optional! If a GUID is not specified, Windows Terminal will generate one for us behind the scenes. The defaultProfile field also accepts a profile's name, for example, "Windows PowerShell 5" or "Ubuntu".

Each profile object in the list array can include settings that apply to that specific shell. If those same settings are moved into the defaults object, they will apply to all shells. The following options are some of the more interesting ones:

- The commandline and source settings control which shell is launched as part of the profile. Only one of these settings should be specified per profile. The commandline setting points to a binary to be executed (for example, powershell.exe or cmd.exe), and is the one we'll use the most often. The source setting contains a reference to a **dynamic profile generator**. These dynamic profile generators are built into Windows Terminal, and contain executable code that looks for shells installed on the system when the terminal is started. For example, the Windows.Terminal.Wsl dynamic profile generator is used to autopopulate the drop-down menu with available WSL2 distributions. We never need to modify this source setting—it's not currently configurable.

- The startingDirectory setting controls which directory is the current working directory when the shell is launched. Setting this to the environment variable, %USERPROFILE%, will default the shell to the C:\Users\{USERNAME} directory. This path should be a Windows path, so for WSL2 profiles, we need to use a UNC path such as \\\\wsl$\\Ubuntu\\home. Note that the backslashes are escaped, as it needs to be a valid JSON string.

- The `hidden` setting controls whether or not the shell appears in the drop-down menu. This option can be useful when temporarily disabling certain profiles. Additionally, as the dynamic profile generators covered previously cannot be deleted, we can use the `hidden` setting to hide any dynamic profiles we are not planning to use. For example, if we don't use Microsoft Azure, we can hide the Azure Cloud Shell using this setting.

The rest of the settings generally deal with UI customization. We'll devote the entire next chapter to UI customization and cover these settings there.

Custom command-line profiles

Windows Terminal's profiles are powerful—we can use any arbitrary program as our shell. Usually, these programs are interactive, but it's not a requirement. In this section, we'll run through a few useful shells that show the power of these custom profiles.

Because each program operates slightly differently, we'll see various useful profile settings for smoothing over these differences to provide uniform access through Windows Terminal.

Git Bash shell

On Windows, Git includes a preconfigured bash shell. We can run this Git Bash shell inside Windows Terminal with the following profile object. The `-li` argument starts our shell as an interactive login shell, so it reads the appropriate start up configuration files:

```
{
  "guid": "{f742cfe1-fa88-4d36-bb67-ac93b526bb80}",
  "name": "Git Bash",
  "commandline": "%PROGRAMFILES%\\Git\\bin\\bash.exe -li",
  "startingDirectory": "%USERPROFILE%",
  "icon": "%PROGRAMFILES%\\Git\\mingw64\\share\\git\\git-for-windows.ico"
}
```

Note that we provided a custom icon resource; the default Git installation conveniently includes an icon file for us:

Figure 4.5 – Git Bash, running inside Windows Terminal

In the preceding screenshot, we can see our custom Git Bash profile running inside Windows Terminal, and our configured icon is in the terminal tab.

SSH shell

In modern development and DevOps environments, we often need to connect to remote systems; SSH is one of the most common ways to connect. As SSH is an interactive program, it's a good fit for Windows Terminal! If SSH is installed and configured on our Windows 10 system, we can use the following profile. If SSH is not installed, see *Chapter 13, Connecting to Remote Systems*, for more details on how to set up a native, Windows Terminal-integrated SSH client:

```
{
    "guid": "{9cc08496-78d7-4d73-8a71-3c8a218e3e2b}",
    "name": "Remote Machine",
    "commandline": "ssh will@example.com"
}
```

If the `screen` command is available on the remote Linux system (it's often installed by default), we can execute `screen` after connecting. This makes the SSH session behave more like Windows Remote Desktop; when we disconnect or close the tab, we can easily reconnect to the same session in a new tab and continue where we left off:

```
{
    "guid": "{9cc08496-78d7-4d73-8a71-3c8a218e3e2b}",
    "name": "Remote Machine",
    "commandline": "ssh -t will@example.com \"screen -x -R\""
}
```

C# interactive shell

Programming language **REPLs** (**Read Eval Print Loops**) are also a good fit for Windows Terminal. Visual Studio ships with **C# Interactive**, and we can configure it as a shell, providing a convenient and fast way to check syntax or class library behavior. The following file paths assume that Visual Studio Professional is installed, but any version of Visual Studio will work as long as the correct file path is provided:

```
{
    "guid": "{c843e9df-48f3-4378-8cc3-0a9e52bcd4e2}",
    "name": "C#",
    "commandline": "%PROGRAMFILES(x86)%\\Microsoft Visual
Studio\\2019\\Professional\\MSBuild\\Current\\Bin\\Roslyn\\csi.
exe",
    "icon": "%PROGRAMFILES(x86)%\\Microsoft Visual Studio\\2019\\
Professional\\Common7\\IDE\\CommonExtensions\\Microsoft\\
ManagedLanguages\\VBCSharp\\LanguageServices\\Interactive\\
Resources\\ScriptFile.ico",
    "closeOnExit": "always"
}
```

We need to specify `"closeOnExit":  "always"` in order to close the terminal tab when C# Interactive exits. This is because the default value of `closeOnExit` is `"graceful"`, which means Windows Terminal only closes the tab when the shell exits with an exit code of zero. As C# Interactive always returns non-zero exit codes, we need to override the default value to compensate:

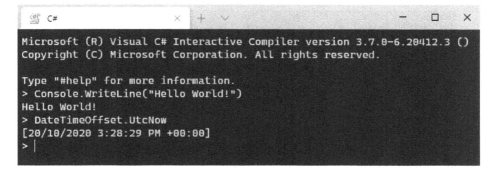

Figure 4.6 – C# Interactive, running inside Windows Terminal

In general, the shell-like nature of REPLs make them a good fit for Windows Terminal; it's handy to have one menu that consolidates our various language REPLs. Next up, let's look at integrating the Node.js REPL.

Node.js interactive shell

Node.js, a JavaScript runtime, also ships with an excellent REPL. Very similar to the preceding C# Interactive profile, we can run node.exe:

```
{
    "guid": "{5a515080-2f71-46ee-82a8-12e58c384ff3}",
    "name": "Node",
    "commandline": "%PROGRAMFILES%\\nodejs\\node.exe"
}
```

Unfortunately, Node.js does not ship with an easily accessible icon file. However, it's easy to extract the icon file from node.exe with the following PowerShell snippet:

```
$exe = "$env:ProgramFiles\nodejs\node.exe"
$output = "$Home\Desktop\node.png"
$icon = [System.Drawing.Icon]::ExtractAssociatedIcon($exe)
$icon.ToBitmap().Save($output)
```

Then, we can move the icon file to the Node.js installation directory and add our "icon" setting in our profile:

```
"icon": "%PROGRAMFILES%\\nodejs\\node.png"
```

Now, when opening Node.js, we can see this icon in our terminal tab:

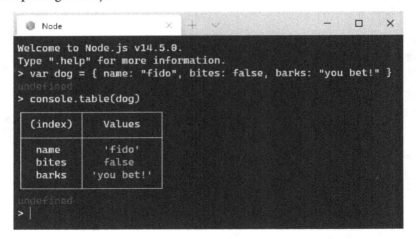

Figure 4.7 – The Node.js REPL running inside Windows Terminal

This particular Node.js icon can also be downloaded from this book's repository mentioned in the beginning of the chapter; but the PowerShell approach can be used to extract icons from any executable.

Next, let's look at something a bit more challenging. We'll add a terminal tab for the terminal that's integrated into the Vim editor!

Vim terminal shell

The Vim editor, as of version 8.1, has an integrated terminal, allowing all the typical Vim commands to be run against the terminal buffer. If the Vim editor is installed (from `https://www.vim.org/download.php`), we can set Vim as our terminal, and execute the "`:term`" command on startup:

```
{
  "guid": "{5a515080-2f71-46ee-82a8-12e58c384ff3}",
  "name": "Vim",
  "commandline": "C:\\tools\\vim\\vim81\\vim.exe -c \"term\"",
  "icon": "C:\\tools\\vim\\vim81\\vim32x32.png",
  "startingDirectory": "%USERPROFILE%"
}
```

Note that we need to use backslashes to escape the quotes in the command-line arguments, similar to how we escape the directory separators.

When we run this, the terminal will open as a Vim split. By pressing *Ctrl* + *W* and then *Shift* + *N*, we can enter Vim mode in the terminal, allowing us to treat the entire terminal buffer as a file in Vim. Pressing *i* for insert mode brings us back to the normal terminal behavior:

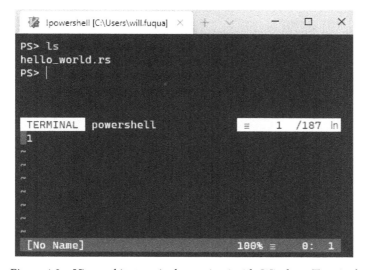

Figure 4.8 – Vim and its terminal, running inside Windows Terminal

Custom profiles provide a convenient way to launch interactive programs, and manage them with Windows Terminal's tabs and panes. Windows Terminal is shaping up to be the one-stop shop for managing our command-line sessions!

Summary

In this chapter, we've taken our first steps into the configuration of Windows Terminal. We discussed the `settings.json` file, which gives us the ability to customize, version control, and share our Windows Terminal configuration.

We've explored the first part of the `settings.json` file, covering the global settings and the per-profile settings. If editing JSON was too painful, no fear: many of these settings are available in the settings UI as well.

We're beginning to see the flexibility and customizability of Windows Terminal through custom profile settings, and we're just getting started! Let's now ramp up our customizations with the next chapter, *Chapter 5, Changing your Windows Terminal appearance.*

5
Changing your Windows Terminal appearance

Continuing our foray into Windows Terminal customization, let's take a deep dive into changing the terminal's appearance. Broadly, there are two main parts to this customization, both of which we'll cover in this chapter: customizing Windows Terminal's UI and color scheme, and shell-specific customizations that use this color scheme.

Customizing the UI and color scheme can be done entirely via the `settings.json` file, which we learned about in the previous chapter. In this chapter, we'll cover the `schemes` section of this file, which controls the color schemes, as well as some custom options in the `profiles` section for changing fonts, translucency, and more. We'll also cover where to download community color schemes, and how to write our own.

When customizing each shell, the steps are a bit more varied; each shell has its own customization options and libraries. We'll cover some useful options and libraries for **PowerShell**, the **WSL2 shell**, and **Command Prompt**.

By the end of this chapter, we will have covered the following areas:

- Terminal color schemes
- Background images and translucency
- PowerShell customization with posh-git, oh-my-posh, and PSReadLine
- WSL2 customization with oh-my-zsh
- Command Prompt customization

Technical requirements

There aren't any technical requirements for this chapter. The configuration files and images referenced in this chapter can be downloaded at `https://github.com/PacktPublishing/Windows-Terminal-Tips-Tricks/tree/main/Chapter 05`.

Terminal color schemes

Anyone who's tried to change their color scheme for the older `conhost.exe` terminal knows that it can be quite painful—the color schemes are split across multiple different files and the registry. Thankfully, in the new Windows Terminal, color schemes are represented by a single JSON object, living in our `settings.json` file. Because these color schemes are simple JSON, it's easy to create and share our own.

Color schemes can also be updated via the Settings UI (*Ctrl + ,*). However, it's easier to download, modify, and share color schemes using JSON, rather than clicking each color individually in the UI. For this reason, we'll be referring to the settings and configuration options by their JSON keys and values throughout this chapter.

Windows Terminal ships with some popular color schemes out of the box, such as **Solarized** and **Tango**. In addition, the easily shareable nature of the color schemes has led to a large community repository. We'll cover both these sources of color schemes, as well as how to write our own in the following sections.

Built-in color schemes

As we discussed in the previous chapter, Windows Terminal ships with a `defaults.json` file (*Ctrl + Alt + ,*). This file defines the following color schemes:

- Campbell
- Campbell Powershell

- Vintage
- One Half Dark
- One Half Light
- Solarized Dark
- Solarized Light
- Tango Dark
- Tango Light

To enable one of the built-in color schemes globally, for all shells, open the `settings.json` file (*Ctrl + Shift + ,*) and set the `profiles.defaults.colorScheme` key to the desired color scheme:

```
"profiles": {
  "defaults": {
    "colorScheme": "Tango Dark"
  },
```

We can also set separate color schemes per shell, for example, to differentiate our WSL2 and PowerShell windows. If we wanted our WSL2 profile specifically to use the *Solarized Dark* color scheme, we could set the `colorScheme` key of that shell's profile:

```
"profiles": {
  "defaults": {
  },
  "list": [
    {
      "guid": "{2c4de342-38b7-51cf-b940-2309a097f518}",
      "name": "Ubuntu",
      "source": "Windows.Terminal.Wsl",
      "colorScheme": "Solarized Dark"
    }
```

After saving the `settings.json` file, Windows Terminal will autoreload and use this color scheme for WSL2 only.

Community-driven color schemes

There are more than 200 Windows Terminal color schemes available on the unofficial *Windows Terminal Themes* website, available at `https://windowsterminalthemes.dev` (GitHub repo: `https://github.com/atomcorp/themes`) and more can be found elsewhere online.

The *Windows Terminal Themes* website provides ports of many popular terminal color schemes, with a preview of each. Let's walk through installing a color scheme from this website. Color schemes from other websites would follow a similar process:

1. Navigate to the preceding website and choose a color scheme. Let's say we've settled on **AtomOneLight**:

Figure 5.1 – Downloading a theme from https://windowsterminalthemes.dev

2. Click **Get theme** to copy the JSON defining this theme to the clipboard.

3. Paste this JSON into the `schemes` array of the `settings.json` file.

4. To activate it, set either the `profiles.defaults.colorScheme` or the `colorScheme` property of a single profile to the name of the color scheme (in our example, `"AtomOneLight"`).

5. Save the `settings.json` file and Windows Terminal will auto-apply the theme.

Next, let's look inside our JSON theme, and learn how to write our own.

Writing your own theme

If none of the preceding color schemes suit our fancy, we can also define our own color scheme. Like most other terminals, Windows Terminal uses the concept of **ANSI color names** for its color scheme. A color scheme is simply a mapping of these ANSI color names to **RGB color values**.

This system of theming uses the standard 16 color names shown in the following JSON. In addition to these 16 color names, Windows Terminal also has 4 additional options for configuring the `background`, `foreground`, `selectionBackground`, and `cursorColor`:

```
{
    "name": "Dracula",
    "background": "#272935",
    "foreground": "#F8F8F2",
    "selectionBackground": "#F8F8F2",
    "cursorColor": "#FFFFFF",
    "black": "#272935",
    "blue": "#BD93F9",
    "cyan": "#6272A4",
    "green": "#50FA7B",
    "purple": "#6272A4",
    "red": "#FF5555",
    "white": "#F8F8F2",
    "yellow": "#FFB86C",
    "brightBlack": "#555555",
    "brightBlue": "#BD93F9",
    "brightCyan": "#8BE9FD",
    "brightGreen": "#50FA7B",
    "brightPurple": "#FF79C6",
    "brightRed": "#FF5555",
    "brightWhite": "#FFFFFF",
    "brightYellow": "#F1FA8C"
}
```

These ANSI color names can be a bit surprisingly named sometimes (for example, *gray* is named `brightBlack`), but by using the standard ANSI color naming conventions, themes for other terminals from Windows, Linux, and macOS can be more easily ported to Windows Terminal.

The additional `background`, `foreground`, `selectionBackground`, and `cursorColor` properties can be overwritten in each profile. This allows us to have subtle variations on the same color scheme across different shells.

We're now done defining our core color scheme for our Windows Terminal color schemes—already it's starting to look good! For the rest of the chapter, we'll cover interesting UI effects available in `settings.json`, and customize our shells to use our color scheme in interesting ways.

Background images and translucency

So far we've covered plain color backgrounds, but Windows Terminal also supports background images. These background images are configured in the `profiles` section, either per profile or in the `defaults` section.

By default, backgrounds fill the entire screen area of Windows Terminal, but this is configurable. For example, let's say we want the friendly GitHub Octocat logo to appear fixed at the bottom right of our terminal, like this:

Figure 5.2 – A background image that only occupies the bottom right of Windows Terminal

This could be accomplished with the following configuration in our `defaults` section:

```
"defaults":
{
    "background": "#282a36",
    "backgroundImage": "C:\\Backgrounds\\Octocat.png",
    "backgroundImageStretchMode": "none",
    "backgroundImageAlignment": "bottomRight",
    "backgroundImageOpacity": 0.8
}
```

The four properties that control how background images are rendered are as follows:

- `backgroundImage` – This is the file path of the image. Animated GIFs are supported!

- `backgroundImageStretchMode` – This specifies how the image should resize to fill the terminal window. There are four values, each illustrated in *Figure 5.3*:

    A. `"uniformToFill"` – Keeps the image aspect ratio and "zooms in" until the image completely fills the window. Parts of the image may be clipped. This is the default value.

    B. `"fill"` – Stretches the image until it fills the window, without preserving the aspect ratio. The image may appear distorted.

    C. `"uniform"` – Scales the image until it fills one axis of the window (vertically or horizontally). The other axis will be filled by the background color.

    D. `"none"` – Does not scale the image.

- `backgroundImageAlignment` – For the preceding `"uniform"` and `"none"` values, this specifies where the image shows in the window. Valid values are strings that represent positions, such as `"left"`, `"bottomLeft"`, `"topRight"`, and so on. The default is `"center"`.

- `backgroundImageOpacity` – This option specifies the opacity of the image, using a decimal value scaled from 0 to 1. At 0, the image will be completely transparent, so only the background color of the color scheme will show through. At 1, the image is completely opaque, covering the background color of the color scheme:

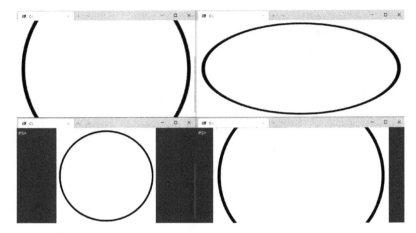

Figure 5.3 – The available stretch modes. The top row shows uniformToFill and fill; the bottom row shows uniform and none

In addition to background-related opacity settings, Windows Terminal also supports translucency, called **acrylic**. This translucency is not full transparency—it provides the artistically blurred see-through effect that is a common Fluent Design element in Windows 10.

To enable acrylic, add the `useAcrylic` and `acrylicOpacity` settings in the `profiles.defaults` object, or in a specific profile section. The following configuration will make Windows Terminal 20% translucent (only 80% opaque):

```
"profiles": {
  "defaults": {
    "useAcrylic": true,
    "acrylicOpacity": 0.8
  }
```

After enabling acrylic with `useAcrylic`, an additional keyboard shortcut is unlocked—holding *Ctrl + Alt + Shift* while scrolling the mouse wheel will make the window more or less translucent, temporarily. When the settings are reloaded or Windows Terminal is restarted, the translucency will be reset back to the `acrylicOpacity` setting.

As our final UI effect, we'll discuss **pixel shaders**. These shaders are miniature computer programs, written in the HLSL shader programming language. These programs can perform advanced graphical effects in Windows Terminal by defining transformations for an individual pixel and then running on every pixel in Windows Terminal. Example pixel shaders, as well as a tutorial for writing them, are available at `https://github.com/microsoft/terminal/tree/main/samples/PixelShaders`.

We can enable pixel shaders in Windows Terminal by using the `experimental.pixelShaderPath` setting, which specifies the file path of the HLSL program. Note that complex pixel shaders may result in reduced performance and battery life!

Now that we've covered the available Windows Terminal color palette and effects, let's take a look at the options available in our various shells: PowerShell, WSL2, and Command Prompt.

Customizing PowerShell with posh-git, oh-my-posh, and PSReadLine

Up until this point, our **PowerShell** prompt has been rather drab, showing only the current working directory. Let's look at the **oh-my-posh** project, a third-party module that provides a way to make our PowerShell prompt both more attractive and useful.

Oh-my-posh can take our default prompt, which looks like this:

Figure 5.4 – The default PowerShell prompt

And turn it into this:

Figure 5.5 – A themed oh-my-posh prompt

This prompt, in addition to standing out from surrounding terminal output, has the following additional features, among many others:

- Supports a rich status display of Git repository state
- Supports many alternate themes
- Shortens longer paths, and supports displaying the home directory as a tilde (~)
- Detects whether the current directory is a **Python virtualenv** or **Anaconda environment**, and displays the name of that environment

- Keeps the terminal tab title synchronized with the current working directory
- Displays a red *x* symbol in the prompt if the previously executed command returned an error status

As of late 2020, oh-my-posh has just completed a major transition from **oh-my-posh version 2** to **oh-my-posh version 3**. PowerShell 5 users should continue to use oh-my-posh version 2, and PowerShell Core users should use version 3. We'll look at both these versions, and cover upgrading to PowerShell Core in *Chapter 8, Tips for Using PowerShell like a Pro*.

Oh-my-posh version 2

First, let's take a look at oh-my-posh version 2. As of late 2020, this is the latest stable version and is compatible with the older **PowerShell 5**:

1. To install oh-my-posh version 2, run the following two PowerShell commands. They will install the `posh-git` module (a prerequisite) and the oh-my-posh module:

   ```
   Install-Module posh-git -Scope CurrentUser
   Install-Module -Name oh-my-posh -RequiredVersion 2.0.496
   ```

2. Download the Cascadia Code fonts from Microsoft, at `https://github.com/microsoft/cascadia-code/releases/latest`. Install all four fonts in the `ttf` subdirectory.

3. In your `settings.json` file (*Ctrl + Shift + ,*), set the `profiles.defaults.fontFace` option to either `"Cascadia Code PL"` or `"Cascadia Mono PL"`. As covered in *Chapter 1, Getting started with the new Windows Terminal*, the former font has special ligatures for programming, whereas the latter does not. Additionally, the `PL` in the font name stands for **Powerline**—the Powerline glyphs are used for rendering the decorative shapes in *Figure 5.5*.

4. Choose a theme. Run `Get-Theme` to get a list of all available themes, and then call `Set-Theme` to choose a theme. For example, `Set-Theme Paradox` or `Set-Theme Agnoster`.

5. Optionally, if there's only one primary user account on the computer, set the `$DefaultUser` variable that username. This will prevent that username from displaying in the prompt.

6. To make the settings apply to new instances of PowerShell, add the following to the PowerShell profile file. This configuration file is separate from Windows Terminal and will modify all future PowerShell windows opened on our system. Open the file by executing `code $profile` from a PowerShell window, and add the following contents:

```
Import-Module posh-git
Import-Module oh-my-posh
$DefaultUser = 'me' # optional line, replace this name
Set-Theme Paradox
```

Done! Now our prompt should be both more functional and better looking!

Oh-my-posh version 3

Oh-my-posh version 3 is a complete rewrite of oh-my-posh v2. Oh-my-posh v3 is written in Go and aims to be usable across multiple shells, including WSL2.

Version 3 drops support for PowerShell 5, and changes from a PowerShell-based configuration to a JSON configuration file. This JSON configuration file can be autogenerated from an existing theme, and then used as a base for further modifications.

Because oh-my-posh v3 is young and rapidly changing, see `https://ohmyposh.dev` for the latest installation instructions and documentation. As of late 2020, the commands to preview and apply themes are as follows:

```
Get-PoshThemes
Set-PoshPrompt -Theme <theme-name> # for example, "agnoster"
```

Themes can be modified by exporting the current theme to a file and then modifying that file. Run the following command to create a new configuration file:

```
Export-PoshTheme -FilePath ~/.oh-my-posh.json
```

Edit this JSON file as desired, in coordination with the documentation available from oh-my-posh's website. The oh-my-posh website has excellent documentation on each configuration option, and a sample oh-my-posh configuration file is available in this book's GitHub repository, linked at the beginning of this chapter.

To make the changes apply to each new PowerShell session, add the following to the PowerShell profile file (open it by running `code $profile` from a PowerShell window):

```
Import-Module oh-my-posh
Set-PoshPrompt -Theme ~/.oh-my-posh.json
```

Don't miss the `osc99` setting! Setting this to `true` will instruct oh-my-posh to notify Windows Terminal when the current directory is changed. This ensures that new Windows Terminal panes have the same starting directory as their parent pane.

Changing the prompt without oh-my-posh

We've covered oh-my-posh in depth because it's the easiest way to get started with a great-looking and functional prompt. However, it's possible to customize the prompt without installing a third-party module, by defining a function named `prompt`. Inside this function, we can call any PowerShell code we want to control both the look and the content of our prompt. In addition, it supports **ANSI escape sequences** for foreground and background colors.

For example, say we wanted to add the current time to our prompt, so we can easily tell when we started a long-running command. Furthermore, let's delineate the current time and the current working directory by making the time a blue-ish color. We could define the `prompt` function as follows:

```
function prompt {
  $brightBlueForeground = "$([char]27)[94m"
  $defaultColor = "$([char]27)[0m"
  $cwd = $executionContext.SessionState.Path.CurrentLocation
  $date = Get-Date -Format "HH:mm:ss"
  "$cwd $brightBlueForeground($date)$defaultColor> "
}
```

Simply defining that function is enough—PowerShell will invoke it for us when it needs to render our prompt. After we define that function in our PowerShell window, our prompt will change into this:

Figure 5.6 – Our PowerShell prompt showing the current time

The tricky part about the preceding function is the ANSI escape sequences. For readability, we put the escape sequences into variables. The **ASCII** code for `Escape` is 27, followed by [nm where n is the number in *Figure 5.7* to change the background or foreground, and m is the literal character "*m*" (which stands for **mode**):

#	Foreground	#		Background			
#	Normal Color	#	Bright Color	#	Normal Color	#	Bright Color
30	Black	90	Bright Black	40	Black	100	Bright Black
31	Red	91	Bright Red	41	Red	101	Bright Red
32	Green	92	Bright Green	42	Green	102	Bright Green
33	Yellow	93	Bright Yellow	43	Yellow	103	Bright Yellow
34	Blue	94	Bright Blue	44	Blue	104	Bright Blue
35	Magenta	95	Bright Magenta	45	Magenta	105	Bright Magenta
36	Cyan	96	Bright Cyan	46	Cyan	106	Bright Cyan
37	White	97	Bright White	47	White	107	Bright White
38	Extended RGB			48	Extended RGB		
39	Default Color			49	Default Color		
0	Reset all formatting to default						

Figure 5.7 – ANSI escape sequences for controlling foreground and background colors

By using these predefined color codes, each color will use the RGB value we specified in our `settings.json` file, so our theme is cohesive. These ANSI escape sequences can take a bit of getting used to; take a moment to review the preceding `$brightBlueForeground` and `$defaultColor` variables, and how they relate to *Figure 5.7*.

While using the standard ANSI escape sequence colors gives us a consistent look, we're not limited to these predefined colors. By using the **Extended RGB** color code (38 for the foreground, 48 for the background in *Figure 5.7*), we can use any RGB value. For example, the syntax for creating an RGB foreground color is the following:

```
"$([char]27)[38;2;(R Value);(G Value);(B Value)m"
```

So, if we wanted to make the foreground a light red color, we could type this:

```
"$([char]27)[38;2;255;200;200m"
```

> **Note**
>
> We're covering the ANSI escape sequences related to color, but there are many more ANSI escape sequences available; see `https://docs.microsoft.com/en-us/windows/console/console-virtual-terminal-sequences#text-formatting` for the full reference.
>
> A particularly useful escape sequence is OSC 9;9, which notifies the Windows Terminal of changes to the current working directory. By putting this escape sequence in our PowerShell `prompt` function, we can ensure that Windows Terminal opens panes with the same working directory as the parent pane. This can be enabled in both PowerShell and WSL2; see `https://gist.github.com/skyline75489/480d036db8ae9069b7009377e6eebb79` for PowerShell and `https://gist.github.com/skyline75489/d655aede4c729eff178a1c0bfd10f622` for WSL2.

If colors aren't enough, we can add emoji, too! If we wanted a snazzy rocketship in our prompt, we just need to add the **Unicode codepoint** for our rocketship to our string:

```
$rocket = [System.Char]::ConvertFromUtf32(0x1F680)
"$cwd $brightBlueForeground($date)$defaultColor $rocket "
```

After redefining our `prompt` function to contain the preceding lines, we'll see the following emoji in our prompt:

Figure 5.8 – Our prompt, rendered with a rocketship emoji

However, keep in mind that while emoji display perfectly in the new Windows Terminal, older terminals like `conhost.exe` will display invalid characters.

After we've defined a prompt we're happy with, we can put it in our PowerShell `$profile` file so it applies to every new PowerShell session. We've now customized our prompt; let's look at customizing the color of commands that we type!

Changing command colors with PSReadline

PSReadline is the built-in PowerShell module that handles many aspects of interacting with the PowerShell prompt, such as autocompletion, keybinding, and more. We'll discuss PSReadline in depth in *Chapter 8, Tips for using PowerShell like a Pro*. For now, let's cover the aspect related to theming: the syntax highlighting of input commands.

When typing a command in PowerShell, PSReadline will highlight the various parts of the command. These parts are called tokens:

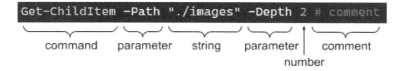

Figure 5.9 – Tokens in a syntax-highlighted PowerShell command

The colors are selected from the color scheme that we set up in our settings.json file earlier in the chapter. However, it's possible to change which colors are selected for which tokens in the command. We can do this with the Set-PSReadlineOption function:

```
Set-PSReadlineOption -Color @{
    "Command" = [ConsoleColor]::Green
    "Parameter" = [ConsoleColor]::Gray
    "Member" = [ConsoleColor]::White
    "Keyword" = [ConsoleColor]::Green
    "Variable" = [ConsoleColor]::White
    "Default" = [ConsoleColor]::White
    "Type" = [ConsoleColor]::Cyan
    "Number" = [ConsoleColor]::Blue
    "String" = [ConsoleColor]::Yellow
    "Operator" = [ConsoleColor]::Magenta
    "ContinuationPrompt" = [ConsoleColor]::White
    "Emphasis" = [ConsoleColor]::Cyan
    "Error" = [ConsoleColor]::Red
    "Comment" = [ConsoleColor]::DarkCyan
}
```

Any color left unspecified won't be changed. Put this command in the PowerShell profile (the file path of which is in the $profile variable) so it runs for each new PowerShell session.

That was quite an intense section, but it shows that PowerShell gives us the flexibility to control every part of the UI. Next, let's discuss customizing WSL2.

WSL2 customization with oh-my-zsh

The same theming configuration that we did for PowerShell is also available for **WSL2**! The settings.json changes will apply automatically; all we need to specify is our prompt. We have three options:

1. **oh-my-posh v3** – This is the same project we covered in the previous section. It's cross-platform!

2. **oh-my-zsh** – This was the original oh-my project, originally released for the **ZSH shell**.

3. **oh-my-bash** – The same as oh-my-zsh but for the **Bash shell**.

As we've already covered option 1 in the previous PowerShell section, we'll now cover option 2, oh-my-zsh. We won't be covering oh-my-bash, as it's very similar to the oh-my-zsh project.

The ZSH shell is a popular, alternative shell for Linux that replaces the default Bash shell. We'll cover it in depth and see the many productivity boosts available in *Chapter 9, Tips for using Ubuntu like an Expert*, but for now, we'll just cover the installation and theming aspects of it.

If you haven't already set up a WSL2 installation, see the instructions in *Chapter 3, Configuring an Ubuntu Linux profile*. We'll be continuing to use Ubuntu in this chapter, but the steps will be very similar regardless of the installed Linux distribution.

Before we can start theming our prompt with oh-my-zsh, we'll install ZSH and start using it:

1. Install ZSH from the package manager. For Ubuntu, it's as follows:

    ```
    sudo apt install zsh
    ```

2. Change from the default Bash shell to ZSH by issuing the **change shell** command:

    ```
    chsh --shell /bin/zsh
    ```

3. After the command completes, open a new WSL2 tab to begin using ZSH! Depending on the Ubuntu version, a **first-run wizard** may launch. Press *q* to exit the wizard—we'll be using the oh-my-zsh configuration instead.

4. Now that we're using the more powerful ZSH shell, we can install oh-my-zsh:

```
sh -c "$(curl -fsSL https://raw.github.com/ohmyzsh/
ohmyzsh/master/tools/install.sh)"
```

The preceding line would be quite long to type out; it can alternatively be copy-pasted from the installation instructions available at `https://ohmyz.sh`.

5. After the installation completes, we can select our theme by opening the `.zshrc` file in our home directory. If you're not sure how to do this, run `code ~/.zshrc`.

6. Select the theme to use by setting the `ZSH_THEME` variable. For example, set `ZSH_THEME="agnoster"`.

Most of the themes from oh-my-posh are also available in oh-my-zsh, which provides a nice, consistent command-line experience:

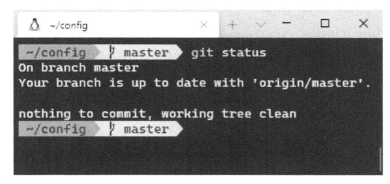

Figure 5.10 – oh-my-zsh on Linux looks very similar to oh-my-posh on PowerShell

We're done with theming ZSH for now, though we've barely scratched the surface of the power of ZSH and oh-my-zsh. As mentioned, we'll dig a bit deeper in *Chapter 9, Tips for Using Ubuntu like an Expert*. For now, let's configure one final shell: Command Prompt.

Command Prompt customization

Command Prompt does not have nearly as many customization options available as PowerShell and ZSH, so this section will be briefer! Luckily, most of our work was done when we set up our `settings.json` earlier in the chapter—Command Prompt will respect those color scheme settings.

The one thing we can customize in Command Prompt is the prompt itself. We can run the `prompt` command to change it temporarily and set the PROMPT environment variable to change it permanently.

The prompt can use ANSI escape sequences similar to the escape sequences we covered as part of the previous PowerShell section. In addition, it has **special variables** for placeholders such as the date and time. Run `prompt /?` to see a list of all available special variables. We'll be using the following special variables:

- $E for color escape codes
- $T for the current time
- $P for the current path
- $C / $F for opening and closing parentheses, respectively
- $G for the "*greater than*" symbol

To recreate our custom "*current time*" prompt that we built in the previous PowerShell section, we could run the following `prompt` command from inside Command Prompt:

```
prompt $P $E[1;94;40m$C$T$F$E[0m$G
```

This renders a prompt like this:

```
C:\Projects (20:40:23.52)>
```

Figure 5.11 – Command Prompt with the current time in the color blue

Again, the ANSI escape sequences are the trickiest part to understand. The color code numbers are the same as the ones in *Figure 5.7* a few pages ago:

- $E[1;94;40m – 94 is the bright blue foreground code; 40 is the black background code.
- $E[0m – 0 is the "*Reset all formatting*" code.

As another exercise, we can even recreate the oh-my-posh agnoster theme, for Command Prompt:

```
prompt $E[1;30;104m►$E[1;37;104m $P $E[1;94;40m►$E[0m
```

This renders as the following:

Figure 5.12 – Command Prompt with an agnoster theme prompt

Here are the color codes broken down:

1. $E[1;30;104m – Set the foreground to black, and the background to bright blue.
2. ▶ – The literal triangle, copy-pasted from the PowerShell agnoster prompt.
3. $E[1;37;104m – Set the foreground to white, and the background to bright blue.
4. $P – The current path, surrounded by spaces.
5. $E[1;94;40m – Set the foreground to bright blue, and the background to black.
6. ▶ – The literal triangle again.
7. $E[0m – The "Reset all formatting" code.

After we've found a prompt we're happy with, we can set the prompt environment variable so it affects new prompts. To set the environment variable, open the **Edit Environment Variable for your Account** option from the Windows 10 Start menu:

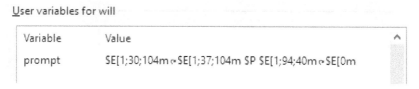

Figure 5.13 – Setting the prompt environment variable to persist changes

The window used for editing environment variable values accepts emoji, and Windows Terminal will display the emoji when running the command prompt. However, the older conhost.exe will not be able to display the emoji characters and will instead render invalid characters.

After setting the environment variable and saving the settings, restart Windows Terminal so it reads the new environment variables.

Summary

We've now covered the UI customization options available for Windows Terminal and its shells. We covered the various settings available in Windows Terminal, ranging from minimalist, flat colors to translucent animated GIF backgrounds.

In addition, we learned how to find and apply community color schemes, and even author our own. We then experimented with using these color schemes from PowerShell, both in the prompt and in the input syntax highlighting. Finally, we learned about oh-my-zsh in WSL2 and studied the arcane art of Command Prompt configuration.

In the next chapter, we'll learn about setting up custom keyboard commands, and sending complex input to automate Windows Terminal at the press of a button!

6
Setting up keyboard shortcuts

In this chapter, we'll cover the final area of the `settings.json`: the `actions` section. This section controls the keyboard shortcuts available in Windows Terminal.

Keyboard shortcuts are mandatory for any well-optimized workflow. In previous chapters, we covered the default keyboard shortcuts, and these will take us quite far. However, Windows Terminal really shines at setting up custom keyboard shortcuts to automate our own command-line tools and layouts.

In this chapter, we'll learn the details of Windows Terminal's keyboard configuration system, and how to set up our own keyboard shortcuts and commands. In addition, we'll explore commands for cycling through terminal window layouts at the press of a button.

We'll cover the following areas:

- Overview of the keyboard shortcut systems
- Building custom commands with `"sendInput"`
- Configuring custom terminal layouts with `"wt"`

Technical requirements

There aren't any technical requirements for this chapter. The configuration options referenced in this chapter can be downloaded from
`https://github.com/PacktPublishing/Windows-Terminal-Tips-Tricks/tree/main/Chapter 06`.

Overview of the keyboard shortcut system

Windows Terminal provides a vast number of **actions** out of the box. These actions are represented by strings that are associated with a programming function in Windows Terminal. For example, the string `"closeWindow"` is associated with a function that will close the terminal window, and the string `"toggleFullscreen"` refers to a function that switches between windowed and fullscreen mode. These actions are represented by JSON objects, in the `"actions"` section of our `settings.json`.

> **Note**
>
> In version 1.3 and earlier of Windows Terminal, this field was named `"keybindings"`. In later versions, it's been renamed to `"actions"` to reflect that associating keyboard shortcuts with each item is not strictly necessary. Both names will continue to work in order to avoid breaking older `settings.json` files.

For example, the `"toggleFullscreen"` action is represented like this:

```
"actions": [
  { "command": "toggleFullscreen" }
]
```

While the preceding command can be referenced in the command palette, we can go one step further and associate it with a keyboard shortcut. We can do this by adding a `"keys"` field inside the object:

```
"actions": [
  { "command": "toggleFullscreen", "keys": "alt+enter" }
]
```

If we wanted to change the keybinding from *Alt + Enter* to *F11*, we could simply update the `"keys"` field, save the file, and Windows Terminal will auto-apply our custom keybinding. If we wanted to have multiple keybindings for a certain action, we could repeat the entire object, varying the `"keys"` field as desired:

```
"actions": [
  { "command": "toggleFullscreen", "keys": "alt+enter" },
  { "command": "toggleFullscreen", "keys": "f11" }
]
```

A full list of available keys that can be bound is available at `https://docs.microsoft.com/en-us/windows/terminal/customize-settings/actions#modifier-keys`. The list includes punctuation, function keys, number pad keys, and "*navigation keys*" such as arrow keys, page up/down, home, and so on.

Some actions can take parameters. For example, the `"splitPane"` action accepts a `"split"` parameter with possible values of `"horizontal"` or `"vertical"`:

```
"actions": [
  { "command": "toggleFullscreen", "keys": "alt+enter" },
  {
    "command": {
      "action": "splitPane",
      "split": "horizontal"
    },
    "keys": "alt+shift+-"
  }
]
```

Notice that when a command does not have parameters, we provide the command as a string (for example, `"toggleFullscreen"`), and when it does have parameters, we provide the command as an object. The string command is simply shorthand; we could also provide the command as an object in either case:

```
"actions": [
  {
    "command": { "action": "toggleFullscreen" },
    "keys": "alt+enter"
  },
  {
    "command": {
      "action": "splitPane",
      "split": "horizontal"
```

```
    },
    "keys": "alt+shift+-"
  }
]
```

So far, we've been using "toggleFullscreen" and "splitPane" in our examples, but there are many more actions available. To find these other actions, we have a couple of options:

- A subset of actions are available in the defaults.json (open it with *Ctrl + Alt + ,*) in the "actions" section towards the bottom of the file.

- All action names can be found via autocomplete in Visual Studio Code. Open the settings.json file, place the text caret in the "command" or "action" field, and press *Ctrl + Space* to trigger autocomplete.

- All actions and their descriptions are documented online at https://docs.microsoft.com/en-us/windows/terminal/customize-settings/actions.

At the time of writing, there are about 40 available keyboard actions available. All the actions we've discussed previously in the book, such as duplicating panes, opening new tabs, and even copy/paste, can be bound to custom keys.

In the remainder of this chapter, we'll cover two of the more powerful actions, both of which give us the ability to hone Windows Terminal into a tool specialized for our specific workflow.

Building custom commands with "sendInput"

One of the most powerful actions available in Windows Terminal is the sendInput command, which was written by a community contributor. This action allows us to send arbitrary keyboard input to our terminal. Let's take a look:

```
{
  "command": {
    "action": "sendInput",
    "input": "cd /projects/\r"
  },
  "keys": "ctrl+alt+p"
}
```

After adding this action, pressing *Ctrl + Alt + p* will automatically navigate to the /
projects/ directory. To accomplish this, the sendInput command simulates typing
on the keyboard; it sends the keystrokes of the characters in the cd /projects/
command to the shell. It then presses *Enter*, as represented by the carriage-return
character \r, to execute the command. We can automate any command that involves
keyboard input!

The sendInput action is ideal for automating frequently executed commands, such as
Git operations, build scripts, or other commands used day to day. sendInput works
independently of the current shell, whether it's **PowerShell**, **Command Prompt**, or
WSL2, giving it an edge over other methods such as shell-specific aliases.

The sendInput action also supports **ANSI input escape sequences** for arrow keys,
delete/backspace, and more. For example, if we wanted to bind *Ctrl + Alt + h* and *Ctrl +
Alt + l* to send left arrow and right arrow keys (reminiscent of Vim-style navigation), we
could add the following settings:

```
{
    "command": {
        "action": "sendInput",
        "input": "\u001b[D"
    },
    "keys": "ctrl+alt+h"
},
{
    "command": {
        "action": "sendInput",
        "input": "\u001b[C"
    },
    "keys": "ctrl+alt+l"
},
```

\u001b is the code for **Escape**, and [D and [C is the code for the left arrow and right
arrow key, respectively. A full list of available input sequences is available in the online
documentation at https://docs.microsoft.com/en-us/windows/console/
console-virtual-terminal-sequences#input-sequences.

Any configured sendInput action is also available in the **Command Palette**. Open the
Command Palette (*Ctrl + Shift + P*) and type either the word send or some part of the
input to find it.

Now that we've covered how to add custom commands that can send arbitrary text inside Windows Terminal, let's look at how to build custom commands that control the terminal user interface itself.

Configuring custom terminal layouts with "wt"

The next action we'll look at is the wt action. The wt action can be used to launch preconfigured tab and pane layouts with the press of a button. For example, let's say we frequently use a certain pane layout when developing a project:

1. A main pane with our editor, for example, vim.

2. A vertical pane with a live-reloading build process, for example, dotnet watch run.

It might look like this:

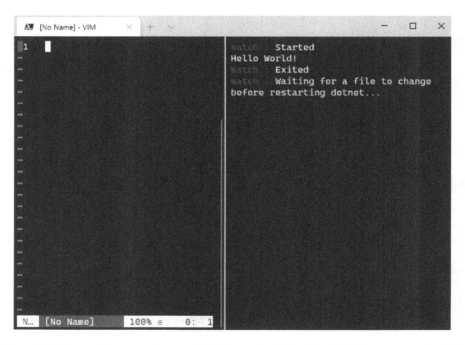

Figure 6.1 – Our custom pane layout, with Vim on the left and our build process on the right

We could manually open panes and launch our editor and build process each time we start working, but that could get tiresome after a while. Windows Terminal supports building these layouts programmatically and associating them with keyboard shortcuts. We do this with the wt action:

```
{
  "command": {
    "action": "wt",
    "commandline": "new-tab -d /projects/MyApp vim; split-pane
-V -d /projects/MyApp dotnet watch run"
  },
  "keys": "ctrl+alt+d"
}
```

In the value of the "commandline" field, we specify two commands, delimited by a semicolon. We first open up a new tab using the new-tab command, with a starting directory of /projects/MyProject/, and run the vim command inside it. Next, we split the pane vertically using split-pane -V, provide the same starting directory, and execute dotnet watch run.

As of late 2020, the wt action is rapidly being updated with more and more capabilities. The best way to find the currently available options is to run the wt --help command from the command line. This command will show a list of supported subcommands (new-tab, split-pane, and focus-tab). Running --help again on each subcommand will show the available flags for that subcommand. At the time of writing, the available options are as follows:

- new-tab – Opens a new tab. Supports the following options:

  A. --profile (-p) <NAME> – The profile to launch. If omitted, it launches the default terminal profile.

  B. --startingDirectory (-d) <DIRECTORY> – The starting directory of the tab. Defaults to the profile default.

  C. --title <TITLE> – The tab title to use for the new tab.

- split-pane – Opens a new pane. It supports all the options of new-tab, plus the following:

  A. --horizontal (-H) – Opens a new pane horizontally.

  B. --vertical (-V) – Opens a new pane vertically.

- `focus-tab` – Moves focus to another tab.

   A. `--target (-t) <INDEX>` – Focuses the tab at the provided index (0-based).

   B. `--previous (-p)` – Changes focus to the tab before the currently focused tab.

   C. `--next (-n)` – Changes focus to the tab after the currently focused tab.

So far we've seen the `new-tab` and `split-pane` subcommands in action; let's see a use case for `focus-tab`. Instead of running our `dotnet watch run` command in a separate pane as we did earlier, let's run it in a background tab. We start a new tab running the `dotnet watch run` command, then chain it with the `focus-tab` command to switch back to our previous tab:

```
{
  "command": {
    "action": "wt",
    "commandline": "new-tab -d /projects/MyApp/ dotnet watch
run; focus-tab -p"
  },
  "keys": "ctrl+alt+d"
},
```

Now, pressing *Ctrl + Alt + d* will start our long-running `dotnet watch run` process in a background tab.

Additional uses of 'wt'

There are two additional ways to use the `wt` command: accessing it from the **command palette**, and when launching a new instance of Windows Terminal.

Windows Terminal exposes all configured `wt` actions via the **command palette**. After configuring a `wt` action as we did in the previous section, open the **command palette** with *Ctrl + Shift + p* and type `run`, or any other part of the configured `wt` command:

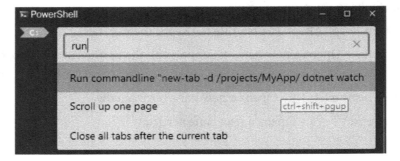

Figure 6.2 – Running a wt action from the command palette

Earlier in the chapter, we discussed how the `"keys"` field is optional. By omitting this field, we could then use the **command palette** as the primary way of accessing our wt actions, without needing to assign and memorize keyboard shortcuts.

> **Note**
>
> If we plan to access an action using the command palette frequently, we can optionally provide `"name"` and `"icon"` fields in the action, which specify a friendly name and icon in the command palette. We can also provide an array of command objects to a new `"commands"` field, to specify nesting in the Command Palette. For more details, see the documentation available at `https://docs.microsoft.com/en-us/windows/terminal/command-palette`.

The wt command can also be used to launch a new Windows Terminal with a specified layout. Windows Terminal ships with a wt.exe binary that supports the same syntax as the wt action. This binary is on the Windows 10 path, so it can be launched from a Windows shortcut, the Windows **Run** dialog, or a command-line shell. The wt.exe binary takes the same options as the wt action:

```
wt new-tab; new-tab; split-pane -H
```

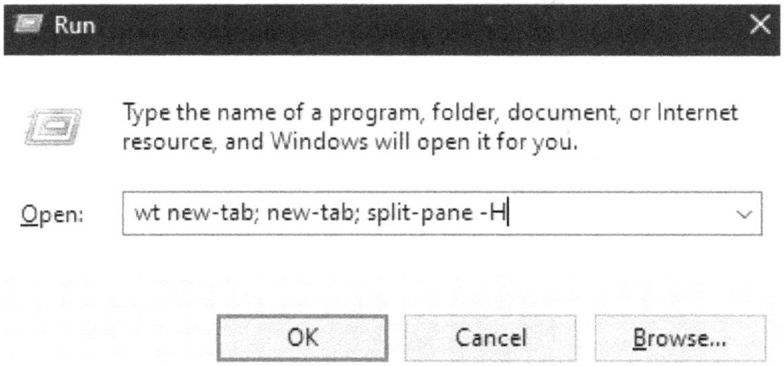

Figure 6.3 – Running wt.exe from the Windows Run dialog

If we're running the command via PowerShell, we need to add special handling for semicolons. Semicolons in the command must be passed to Windows Terminal for processing; this means that they should be escaped with backticks when the command is run under PowerShell, where the semicolon has a special meaning:

```
wt new-tab`; new-tab`; split-pane -H
```

By using the `wt.exe` command, we can easily set up **Desktop** or **Start** menu shortcuts for launching customized Windows Terminal layouts. For example, we could have a frontend development terminal layout that specializes in our npm-based development. This is an exciting part of Windows Terminal, and we can look forward to more enhancements in this system in the future.

> **Note**
>
> For more examples of how to use the `wt.exe` command, see `https://docs.microsoft.com/en-us/windows/terminal/command-line-arguments?tabs=windows`.

Summary

In this chapter, we've done a deep dive into the various keybinding options available in Windows Terminal.

We started out with the built-in Windows Terminal commands and learned about the structure of adding actions, passing parameters, and associating them with keybindings.

We then learned how to send arbitrary input to our shells using the `sendInput` command. This enabled us to rapidly perform tasks across multiple shells, like changing to common directories or running frequently-used Git commands.

Finally, we discussed the `wt` command, which allowed us to create custom commands for manipulating Windows Terminal's tabs and panes. This same technique could be used when launching Windows Terminal via command-line parameters.

This chapter has served as our introduction to **actions** in Windows Terminal. In the next chapter, we'll investigate some useful but hidden actions available in Windows Terminal.

7
Hidden Windows Terminal Actions

Windows Terminal contains a set of **actions** that are *hidden by default*—that is, not bound to any keyboard shortcut and not listed in the `settings.json` file. In this chapter, we'll learn how to discover these actions and cover some of the more interesting actions available.

This set of actions changes over time; it increases as the developers from Microsoft and the open source community create new actions and decreases as actions prove popular enough to get an associated keyboard shortcut. In this chapter, we'll cover the actions that are hidden as of December 2020, and provide instructions on how to identify more hidden actions added in the future.

We'll cover the following areas in this chapter:

- Discovering unbound actions
- Using actions for focus management
- Using actions for visual effects
- Using actions for tab manipulation

Technical requirements

This chapter does not have any technical requirements—having an up-to-date Windows Terminal installation is enough. All the configuration options we discuss in this chapter are available on GitHub at `https://github.com/PacktPublishing/Windows-Terminal-Tips-Tricks/tree/main/Chapter 07`.

Discovering unbound actions

The hidden actions in Windows Terminal can be hard to find. Ultimately, as Windows Terminal is open source, we can always read through the source code to find them, but that is a lengthy process given the number of actions involved. Most of these actions are listed in the **command palette**, but it's hard to discover them if we don't know what to type!

The first stop for finding actions should be Microsoft's documentation, available at `https://docs.microsoft.com/en-us/windows/terminal/customize-settings/actions`. The Windows Terminal team does a great job of keeping this up to date. However, even this documentation doesn't list all the actions available.

Luckily, Windows Terminal ships with a **JSON schema**. The schema is used to validate that the `settings.json` file is well-formed, and also to power Visual Studio Code's autocompletion.

The JSON schema file can be found by opening `settings.json` (*Ctrl + Shift + ,*) and navigating to the `$schema` field toward the top of the file. The value of this field is a hyperlink. Hold *Ctrl* while clicking the link to open it in the browser:

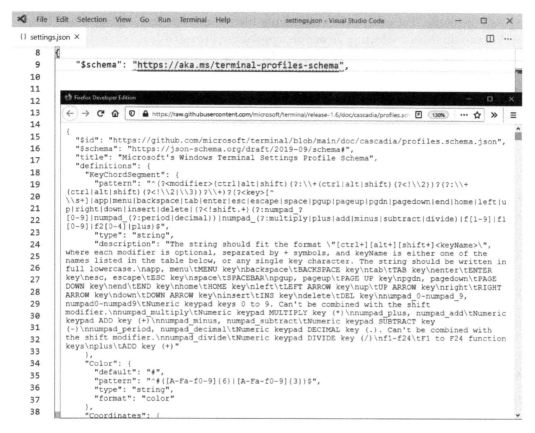

Figure 7.1 – Left: the "$schema" field in the settings.json file. Right: the JSON schema document

This file is a large, complex JSON document clocking in at over 1,000 lines. We are most interested in the `ShortcutActionName` field. Find it in the JSON document and examine the field's array value. These are all the supported actions, hidden and otherwise:

```
"ShortcutActionName": {
  "enum": [
    "adjustFontSize", "closeOtherTabs", "closePane", "closeTab", "closeTabsAfter",
    "closeWindow", "commandPalette", "copy", "duplicateTab", "find", "moveFocus",
    "newTab", "nextTab", "openNewTabDropdown", "openSettings", "openTabColorPicker",
    "paste", "prevTab", "renameTab", "resetFontSize", "resizePane", "scrollDown",
    "scrollDownPage", "scrollUp", "scrollUpPage", "sendInput", "setColorScheme",
    "setTabColor", "splitPane", "switchToTab", "tabSearch", "toggleAlwaysOnTop",
    "toggleFocusMode", "toggleFullscreen", "togglePaneZoom", "toggleRetroEffect",
    "wt", "unbound"
  ],
  "type": "string"
},
```

Figure 7.2 – The ShortcutActionName field in the JSON schema document. Actions are added to this list as new versions of Windows Terminal are released

That's half the battle. The other half is to identify the **parameters** that a given action has, if any. We can do this by selecting an action, appending the word Action to the action's name, and searching for the result. For example, let's choose an interesting action such as setColorScheme. Appending the word Action gives us setColorSchemeAction, which we can then find in the file:

```
"SetColorSchemeAction": {
  "description": "Arguments corresponding to a Set Color Scheme Action",
  "allOf": [
    { "$ref": "#/definitions/ShortcutAction" },
    {
      "properties": {
        "action": { "type": "string", "pattern": "setColorScheme" },
        "colorScheme": {
          "type": "string",
          "default": "",
          "description": "the name of the scheme to apply to the active pane"
        }
      }
    }
  ],
  "required": [ "colorScheme" ]
},
```

Figure 7.3 – The parameter definition for the setColorScheme action

This shows us that the setColorScheme action requires a colorScheme parameter, which represents the name of the scheme to apply to the active pane.

As another example, let's do the same thing for toggleShaderEffects. After searching for toggleShaderEffectsAction, we find nothing, so we know there are no parameters for this command.

Now that we know how to find hidden actions from the JSON schema file, let's cover a list of hidden actions as of December 2020.

Using actions for focus management

When we're using Windows Terminal, the last thing we want is to get distracted by managing the terminal itself! Ideally, the terminal is a tool that helps us accomplish our tasks, not obstruct them. The next three commands help Windows Terminal get out of our way so we can focus on the task at hand.

togglePaneZoom

In *Chapter 2*, *Learning the Windows Terminal UI*, we covered using panes to accomplish multiple Terminal tasks in the same tab. Sometimes, a pane needs to be expanded temporarily in order to see more terminal output. In *Figure 7.4*, we can see two panes in the back window, and the text in the right-side pane is wrapping and difficult to read. By toggling pane zoom, as shown in the front window, we can temporarily expand the right-side pane to fill the full window. This gives us more room so the text doesn't need to wrap, making it easier to read. Toggling pane zoom again will restore the two-pane layout:

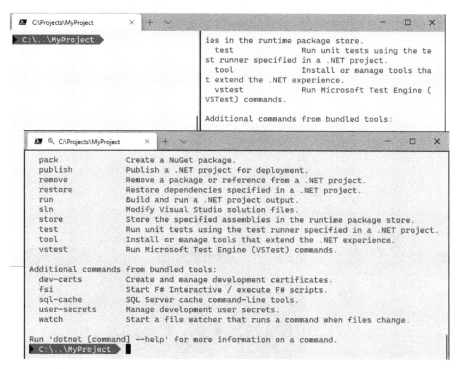

Figure 7.4 – Back: a narrow pane with wrapped text. Front: the pane zoomed to the full window width. Note the magnifying glass in the tab title, representing the zoom

This is an incredibly useful command and well worth a keyboard shortcut. Let's set it up to be *Alt* + *Shift* + *Z*. This follows the existing convention of the *Alt* key managing all pane-related keyboard shortcuts:

```
{
  "command": "togglePaneZoom",
  "keys": "alt+shift+z"
},
```

Now, we don't need to worry about micromanaging our pane size; we can toggle pane zoom on and off to get the job done!

toggleAlwaysOnTop

`toggleAlwaysOnTop` is a useful feature that will keep the Windows Terminal on top of other windows, even if those other windows have focus. This is helpful when using Windows Terminal in conjunction with documentation, and avoids the need to *Alt + Tab* between windows, or resize windows to prevent overlapping:

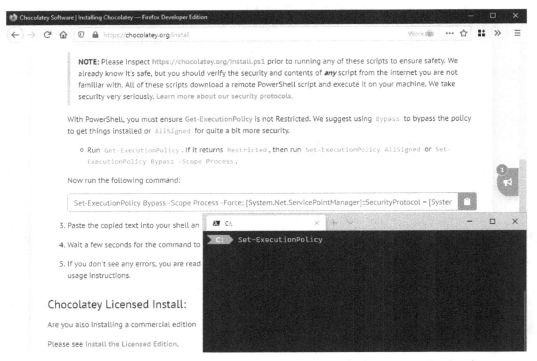

Figure 7.5 – A terminal pinned on top of all other windows. The browser window has focus

We can pin Windows Terminal to the top of the screen, so it's always on top of the other windows, by pressing *Ctrl + Alt + P* after adding the following setting:

```
{
  "command": "toggleAlwaysOnTop",
  "keys": "ctrl+alt+p"
},
```

As this is a toggle, pressing *Ctrl + Alt + P* will enable always-on-top mode, and pressing it again will disable it.

toggleFocusMode

Windows Terminal supports a **focus mode**, which hides all the UI elements except for the shell window. This provides an attractive, distraction-free terminal environment:

Figure 7.6 – A terminal in focus mode. The tabs and window controls are hidden

We can bind this to the *F12* key (similar to *F11*, our shortcut for fullscreen) with the following setting:

```
{
  "command": "toggleFocusMode",
  "keys": "f12"
},
```

We've now covered all the window and pane management actions available as of December 2020. However, the Windows Terminal team is frequently adding more.

Next up, let's cover a couple of actions for controlling visual effects.

Using actions for visual effects

Windows Terminal currently has several hidden commands for managing visual effects. These commands are likely to be used rarely, but let's explore them anyway.

setColorScheme

From our example at the beginning of the chapter, we found that `setColorScheme` is an available action, with a `colorScheme` parameter. It does not have an associated keyboard shortcut. If we wanted to change our Windows Terminal color scheme with a keyboard shortcut (for example, *Ctrl + Alt + S*), we could add the following configuration:

```
{
  "command": {
    "action": "setColorScheme",
    "colorScheme": "Solarized Light"
  },
  "keys": "ctrl+alt+s"
},
```

This can be useful to switch between the light and dark modes of the same theme, for example, **Solarized Light** and **Solarized Dark**. Each theme could be associated with a separate keyboard shortcut. When using a terminal in low light conditions, dark mode is easier on the eyes; in high glare conditions, light mode is easier to read.

toggleShaderEffects

`toggleShaderEffects`, also covered in our earlier example, applies a pixel shader effect. The default shader effect emulates CRT monitor scanlines in the terminal, but we can provide any shader effect we want (even our own custom shaders) by specifying the `experimental.pixelShaderPath` setting:

Figure 7.7 – Left: a normal terminal. Right: the terminal with shader effects

Some people may find this hard to read, so rather than showing an example keyboard shortcut, we'll take the opportunity to use it from the command palette. Press *Ctrl + Shift + P* to open the command palette, and type `visual effects`:

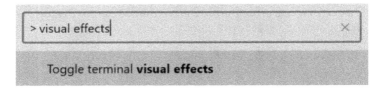

Figure 7.8 – The command palette showing the toggleShaderEffects action

Now, whenever we're feeling nostalgia for old-school computing, we can enable this retro effect mode.

Using actions for tab manipulation

Windows Terminal has several tab manipulation commands that are not yet available in the UI. These commands are likely to be added to menus in the near future, but we can discover and use them before that happens.

Closing multiple tabs at once

Similar to browser tab management, Windows Terminal supports closing multiple tabs at once:

- `closeTabsAfter` will close all tabs after the currently active tab:

```
{
  "command": "closeTabsAfter",
  "keys": "ctrl+shift+delete"
},
```

- `closeOtherTabs` will close all but the currently active tab:

```
{
  "command": "closeOtherTabs",
  "keys": "ctrl+shift+backspace"
},
```

By binding these actions to keyboard shortcuts, we're able to access them even though they're not currently available in the UI!

Changing tab colors

`openTabColorPicker` will open a color picker that can change the color of the current tab. While it's not a frequently accessed action, we can use it to highlight certain tabs as *dangerous*. For example, we could color a tab connected to a production server as red:

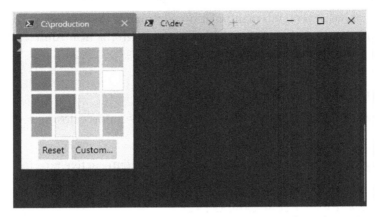

Figure 7.9 – The color picker launched by the openTabColorPicker action

While binding this action to a key is possible, we can also access it via the command palette by pressing *Ctrl + Shift + P* and typing `set the tab color`. The *Tab* key will cycle through the available colors, and pressing *Enter* will select a color.

Summary

In this chapter, we learned how to use the JSON schema to find all the possible actions available in Windows Terminal. We covered the currently hidden commands as of 2020, including commands for visual effects, focus management, and tab manipulation.

At this point, we've covered all the major areas of Windows Terminal. In the next chapter, and the remainder of the book, we'll focus on using shells such as PowerShell and WSL2 to their fullest potential.

8
Tips for using PowerShell like a Pro

Up until this point in the book, we've focused on using Windows Terminal to its fullest potential. From this point on, we'll switch focus to mastering the shells inside Windows Terminal. In this chapter, we will fine-tune **PowerShell**, the most popular shell on Windows 10, into a first-class command-line experience. Future chapters will focus on **WSL2** and performing common frontend, backend, and DevOps tasks efficiently.

There are two parts to PowerShell: the command-line shell and the full-featured scripting language. In this chapter, we will cover only the command-line shell portion. We will not cover the scripting language in depth as it is a large topic that could fill multiple books (and has!).

We'll cover the following topics in this chapter:

- Installing PowerShell Core
- Using built-in commands and aliases
- Configuring PSReadLine in PowerShell Core

- Adding GNU coreutils to the path
- Installing the z utility

Technical requirements

In this chapter, we'll require at least Windows 10 version 17763, as reported by the `winver` command. This version of Windows 10 was released in October 2018. The PowerShell configuration options we discuss in this chapter are available online at `https://github.com/PacktPublishing/Windows-Terminal-Tips-Tricks/tree/main/Chapter 08`.

Installing PowerShell Core

The first step to using PowerShell is to upgrade it! By default, Windows 10 comes with Windows PowerShell 5, while the latest version is **PowerShell Core version 7**. PowerShell Core is a modern, fast, and open source version of PowerShell, and was initially released in August 2016. It's now a stable, complete alternative to Windows PowerShell 5.

PowerShell Core runs alongside Windows PowerShell 5, so there's no risk to installing it. Windows PowerShell 5 can still be used to run any existing, older scripts, while PowerShell Core can be used as the day-to-day shell in Windows Terminal.

PowerShell Core has several benefits over Windows PowerShell 5:

- **Cross-platform and open source**: In addition to Windows, PowerShell Core works on both macOS and Linux and is MIT licensed.

- **Faster performance**: Both initialization and module loading are faster. Anecdotally, shell initialization is almost twice as fast as PowerShell 5.

- **More language and shell features**: PowerShell Core has several features, both in the core language and in the shell commands, that make life easier for users.

PowerShell Core can be installed in two ways, either from the **Microsoft Store** (the app is named *PowerShell*) or downloaded from GitHub at `https://github.com/PowerShell/PowerShell/releases/latest`. When downloading from GitHub, there are many download options for various platforms; download and run the installer ending in `win-x64.msi`:

Figure 8.1 – Running the win-x64 PowerShell Core installer

> **Note**
> Users of **winget**, the command-line installer from Microsoft that's currently in preview, can install PowerShell Core with the `winget install --name PowerShell --exact` command.

After finishing the installation, restart Windows Terminal. Windows Terminal will auto-discover PowerShell Core and add it to the *new shell drop-down menu*, as seen in *Figure 8.2*. There are two PowerShell options available: **PowerShell** is our new PowerShell Core and **Windows PowerShell** is the older version, still available to support any legacy scripts we may have:

Figure 8.2 – PowerShell (Core) and the older Windows PowerShell 5 are available side by side

From here on out, we'll be using PowerShell Core in Windows Terminal. Many of our productivity tips will still work on Windows PowerShell 5, but some will not. Installing PowerShell Core is highly recommended.

Let's set PowerShell Core to be our default profile in Windows Terminal. Open the `settings.json` file (*Ctrl + Shift + ,*) and find the `Windows.Terminal.PowershellCore` profile. For example, it might look like this:

```
{
    "guid": "{574e775e-4f2a-5b96-ac1e-a2962a402336}",
    "hidden": false,
    "name": "PowerShell",
    "source": "Windows.Terminal.PowershellCore",
}
```

Take the value of the `name` field and copy it into the `defaultProfile` field at the top of the `settings.json` file:

```
"defaultProfile": "PowerShell",
```

Now, when we start Windows Terminal or open new tabs, it will default to our new PowerShell Core installation. Let's look at how we can use PowerShell Core like a pro.

Using built-in commands and aliases

In this section, we'll review some useful commands built into PowerShell Core. These commands will work on any PowerShell Core installation and will increase the speed that we can operate on the command line.

Automatic Variable: $^ and $$

In PowerShell Core (and the older PowerShell 5), the **automatic variables** $^ and $$ always contain the first and last word of the previous command, respectively. PowerShell keeps this variable up to date as we issue commands. For example, let's create a new directory and then navigate into it using the $$ variable:

```
> cd ~/Desktop
> mkdir SubDir
> cd $$
```

Rather than retyping the name of the new directory, we can use the $$ variable. When executing the `cd $$` command, the $$ variable represents the last word of the previous command, that is, `SubDir`. This changes the directory to `SubDir`.

Next, let's look at the $^ variable, which contains the first word of the previous command. We can use it to look up help for a previously issued command:

```
> Get-ChildItem -Attributes
Get-ChildItem: Missing an argument for parameter 'Attributes'.
> help $^
```

In our first command, we tried to execute `Get-ChildItem`, but we received an error. Next, we executed the `help $^` command, where $^ represents the first word of the previous command, that is, `Get-ChildItem`. This opens the help for the `Get-ChildItem` command.

We can use these automatic variables to reduce our typing; whenever we want to issue a command related to a previous command, these variables can come into play.

cd - and cd +

On PowerShell Core, the `cd` command supports the - and + optional arguments for navigating backward and forward through our previously visited directories.

For example, let's navigate to the `Desktop` directory, create a directory named `SubDir`, and then use `cd -` and `cd +` to jump back and forth between the `Desktop` and `SubDir` directories:

```
> cd ~/Desktop
> mkdir SubDir
> cd $$
> cd -
> cd +
```

The first `cd -` will navigate us back to our desktop, and the following `cd +` will navigate us forward to `SubDir`. We can repeat `cd -` and `cd +` as often as we want; PowerShell automatically keeps track of both the history of visited directories and our current index in this history.

The ii command

The `Invoke-Item` command, with an alias of `ii`, will open the supplied file or directory in the default application for its file type. This command respects the applications selected in the **Default Apps** settings in Windows 10.

From the command line, we often want to open the current directory in Windows Explorer. Rather than renavigating to the directory in Windows Explorer, a simple `ii .` command will open Windows Explorer directly. It's even faster than typing `explorer .` and has the additional benefit of working with other file types:

- Directories open in Windows Explorer

- Images open in the default image viewer

- JSON files open in the default JSON editor, such as Visual Studio Code

- HTML files open in the default browser, such as Firefox

- Application-specific files open in that application (for example, SLN files will open in Visual Studio)

The `Invoke-Item` command should be our go-to command whenever we want to open a file or directory in an application.

History navigation with h and r

The commands `Get-History` and `Invoke-History`, with aliases of `h` and `r`, respectively, can be used to quickly show previous shell commands and run them.

The `h` command will show a list of all previously executed commands, their duration, and an integer ID:

```
Id      Duration CommandLine
--      -------- -----------
1          0.072 cd ~/Desktop/Project
2          0.601 npm run build
3          0.056 rm -r node_modules
4          0.596 npm run build
```

Figure 8.3 – Our previous command history, as shown by the "h" command

The `r` command takes an integer ID and runs the command associated with that ID. In *Figure 8.3*, the `r 3` command would run the `rm -r node_modules` command. As we execute commands, they're appended to the history with an incremented ID. This means that the IDs are stable; in the current session, `r 3` will always execute the same `rm -r node_modules` command.

If our history becomes too long and messy to manage, we can clear our history with the `Clear-History` command, which is aliased to `clhy`.

Being able to rerun commands is an important part of mastering the command line. We'll see additional ways of interacting with our history later in the chapter.

Pipelines and $_

Chaining multiple commands into a **pipeline** is a crucial part of every shell; by composing multiple smaller commands into a larger command, we can build advanced functionality from simple components. Like most shells, PowerShell uses the pipe operator (represented by the | character) to build pipelines; it passes the output of one command as the input of the next command. For example, if we wanted to list the items in the current directory, sorted by when each item was last updated, we don't need a custom command; we can simply compose two more general commands into the pipeline:

```
Get-ChildItem | Sort-Object LastWriteTime -Descending
```

The preceding `Get-ChildItem` command will generate a list of items (that is, files and directories) in the current directory, and these items are then *piped* to the `Sort-Object` command. The `Sort-Object` command then sorts the items by their `LastWriteTime` property, in descending order.

Additionally, if we wanted to list all system processes by their memory usage, we could run the following:

```
Get-Process | Sort-Object WorkingSet -Descending
```

This demonstrates some of the power of pipelines: we accomplished two different tasks, but reused the general `Sort-Object` command; we didn't need special sorting support in `Get-ChildItem` or `Get-Process` and didn't need to memorize separate command-line flags.

Additionally, this shows how PowerShell passes structured objects through pipes; the `Sort-Object` command takes a property name of the object as the first parameter. This allows for cleaner, more structured code; we don't need to parse lines of text like in other shell languages (notably GNU Bash and Windows batch files).

We're also not limited to chaining together existing commands; we can chain together arbitrary PowerShell code using **script blocks**, that is, PowerShell code enclosed in curly braces. Like the built-in commands, script blocks are called for each object passed through the pipeline. Inside a script block, the "current" object being processed is represented by the $_ automatic variable:

```
Get-ChildItem | Where-Object { $_.LastWriteTime -gt (get-date
2021-01-01) }
```

In the preceding command, we are getting a list of all files and directories that were updated after January 1st, 2021. We're using the general `Where-Object` command to do the filtering, by providing a script block that tests whether `LastWriteTime` is greater than January 1st. `Where-Object` is called for each object returned by `Get-ChildItem`, and only returns the objects that satisfy the condition in the script block.

Pipelines and the $_ automatic variable provide a powerful way to build up ad hoc command chains to quickly accomplish our goals. To learn more, check out the PowerShell overview available at `https://docs.microsoft.com/en-us/powershell/scripting/overview`.

Custom Profile Aliases and Functions

PowerShell supports defining **custom aliases** and **functions**, both of which can reduce our typing at the command line.

Custom aliases are a way to provide alternate, shorter names for commands. If we often use the Visual Studio Code editor; for example, we could alias `code` to `c` by putting the following in our PowerShell `$profile`:

```
Set-Alias -Name c -Value code
```

This allows us to type `c .` and open the current directory in Visual Studio Code.

> **Note**
>
> As a refresher, the PowerShell `$profile` is a file that runs at the start of every PowerShell session and is used to configure that session. It's not part of Windows Terminal, but part of PowerShell itself. Type `$profile` at the command line to see the path of the file (if it doesn't exist, create it). Alternatively, type `code $profile` to launch Visual Studio Code and edit the file directly.

We can automate longer commands, or sets of commands, by wrapping them in a function. The following function navigates to our project directory, opens Visual Studio Code, and refreshes the Git metadata from our remotes. After putting this function in our $profile, we can type work at the command line to invoke it:

```
function work() {
    cd C:\Projects\MyProject\
    code .
    git fetch --all
}
```

Like other languages, PowerShell functions support **parameters**. Right now, our work function hardcodes the MyProject directory. Realistically, we'll have many projects, so we could parameterize the function to accept any directory:

```
function work($dir) {
    cd $dir
    code .
    git fetch --all
}
```

Now, we can type work .\path\to\project to begin working on any project.

PowerShell is a full-featured language and has many options for automation. We've barely scratched the surface of PowerShell as a language; for more information, see the official documentation at https://docs.microsoft.com/en-us/powershell/.

Configuring PSReadLine in PowerShell Core

The **PSReadLine** PowerShell module is critical to set up. It controls many aspects of the command-line editing experience, including accepting input, providing hotkeys, and various algorithms for autocompletion. It strives to provide a good experience out of the box and provides many configuration settings for fine-tuning its behavior.

PSReadLine is so important that Windows 10 started bundling it as part of PowerShell. However, the bundled version can quickly get out of date, and it's worth updating to get the newest features and fixes.

In this section, we'll update the PSReadLine module and install two additional modules: `posh-git` and `oh-my-posh`. We covered all three of these modules from a UI and theming perspective in *Chapter 5, Changing your Windows Terminal appearance*; in this section, we'll dive deeper into the features that PSReadLine provides. As a summary, these three modules can be activated in PowerShell Core with the following steps:

1. Install `posh-git` and `oh-my-posh`:

    ```
    Install-Module -Name posh-git -Scope CurrentUser
    Install-Module -Name oh-my-posh -Scope CurrentUser
    Install-Module -Name PSReadLine -AllowPrerelease -Scope
    CurrentUser -Force -SkipPublisherCheck
    ```

    The `-SkipPublisherCheck` flag allows us to upgrade the older, bundled version of PSReadLine to the latest version from the **PowerShell Gallery**.

2. Add the following commands to the `$profile` file:

    ```
    Import-Module PSReadLine
    Import-Module posh-git
    Import-Module oh-my-posh
    Set-PoshPrompt
    ```

PSReadLine has a wealth of features for supercharging and configuring our PowerShell editing experience. There are two PowerShell commands we'll be calling:

*   `Set-PSReadLineOption`: This command exposes all the options available in PSReadLine in a convenient, autocomplete-capable interface. Each available option is a separate command-line flag.

*   `Set-PSReadLineKeyHandler`: This command allows us to associate keyboard shortcuts with a PowerShell prompt action.

Let's take a look at how we can use these two commands to configure PSReadLine. These commands have many different options, so we'll only be covering the most important and impactful ones.

EditMode

The first option we'll cover is the PSReadLine `EditMode`. It has three possible values:

```
Set-PSReadLineOption -EditMode Windows
Set-PSReadLineOption -EditMode Vi
Set-PSReadLineOption -EditMode Emacs
```

By default, PSReadLine uses `-EditMode Windows`. This mode follows the typical Visual Studio and PowerShell keyboard shortcuts. For example, with `-EditMode Windows`, we can select and copy the prompt's input text with *Ctrl + A* (select all) and *Ctrl + C* (copy). This is a nice, logical mode to get started with.

In `Emacs` mode, the keyboard shortcuts match those of the **Bash shell** (which in turn match the **Emacs editor**). When using `Emacs` mode, the *Ctrl + A* keyboard shortcut would jump to the beginning of the line. For those who are more comfortable with Bash, this is the option to choose.

Finally, the `Vi` mode emulates the modal editing behavior of the **Vi/Vim editor**. Pressing *Esc* will enter **normal mode**, where the typical Vim commands for manipulating text take effect. Vim users will feel at home with this option.

It's possible to mix and match these keyboard shortcuts. For example, with the `Vi` mode, we might still want to use *Ctrl + A* to select all text. After setting `-EditMode Vi`, we can then selectively enable selecting text with the following:

```
Set-PSReadLineKeyHandler -Key Ctrl+a -Function SelectAll
```

At the end of the chapter, we'll have a complete PowerShell `$profile` showcasing additional `Set-PSReadLineKeyHandler` commands for selectively enabling editing operations.

History Search

As we covered earlier in the chapter, we can view our history and rerun commands from the history using the h and r aliases for `Get-History` and `Invoke-History`, respectively. However, PSReadLine supports a faster, more interactive way of doing so.

Say we issued the following commands in a Git repository, where we looked at the current Git repository status and then copied two files into the repository:

```
git status
cp ~/index.html .
cp ~/about.html .
```

Now, we want to run the `git status` command again. After enabling **history search** in PSReadline, we could simply press *g* and then the up arrow. It would autocomplete our command line with the matching `git status` line from our history. Pressing the up arrow additional times would autocomplete with lines further back in the history:

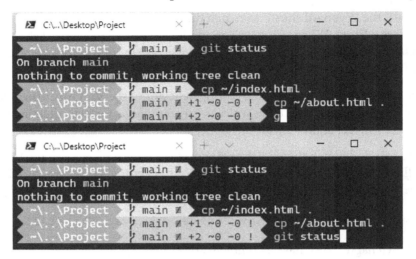

Figure 8.4 – Top: the terminal before we press the up arrow. Bottom: after pressing the up arrow

We can enable this feature by adding the following three lines of configuration to our PowerShell `$profile` file:

```
Set-PSReadLineKeyHandler -Key UpArrow -Function
HistorySearchBackward
Set-PSReadLineKeyHandler -Key DownArrow -Function
HistorySearchForward
Set-PSReadLineOption -HistorySearchCursorMovesToEnd
```

This history search is the most common way of re-running commands from history, but it has a downside: we need to remember the beginning of the command. However, if we can't remember the beginning of the command, we're still in luck: PSReadLine supports searching for substrings of previous commands.

Using our previous example, let's say we only remembered the `status` part of `git status`. We can press *Ctrl + R* to bring up the `find:` prompt as seen in *Figure 8.5*, type our matching substring (`status`), and press *Enter* to populate our prompt with the matching `git status` command:

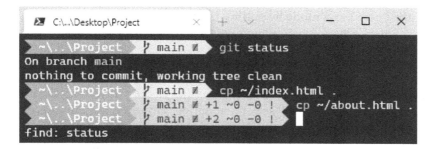

Figure 8.5 – Ctrl + R being used to search our history for a command containing the word "status."
Depending on PSReadline's configuration, it may say "bck-i-search" instead of "find"

The *Ctrl + R* feature is enabled by default; there's no special configuration needed to access it.

Better autocompletion

By default, when we press *Tab*, PowerShell will **autocomplete** our command with the best matching option. Pressing *Tab* again will cycle through any additional matching options. However, this can sometimes be painful, because we're not sure how many times we'll need to press *Tab* to get to the option we want; it could be 3 more times, or it might be 30.

PSReadLine provides two additional modes for autocompletion: `Complete` and `MenuComplete`. The `Complete` mode will be more comfortable for those used to the Bash shell. Most other users, including those who use **Zsh**, will like the `MenuComplete` mode more.

The `Complete` mode provides Bash-style autocompletion. When pressing *Tab* to autocomplete a line, if there's only one possible option, this mode will select that option. If there's more than one option, it will print all the options and then draw a new prompt on the next line:

Figure 8.6 – Bash-style "Complete" mode prints the available options and draws a new prompt

We can select the `Complete` mode by putting the following line in our PowerShell `$profile`:

```
Set-PSReadLineKeyHandler -Key Tab -Function Complete
```

The `MenuComplete` mode is more interactive. Similar to the previous mode, if only one option is possible, this mode will select that option. However, if there is more than one possible option, it will print a navigable menu containing all the options, and typing additional text will filter down the options in the menu. Additionally, the arrow keys may be used to navigate the menu and manually select an option:

Figure 8.7 – MenuComplete mode draws a navigable and filterable menu of completions

To use the `MenuComplete` mode, add the following line to the PowerShell `$profile`:

```
Set-PSReadLineKeyHandler -Key Tab -Function MenuComplete
```

To see the changes take effect, open a new Windows Terminal PowerShell tab, type a few characters of a command, and press the *Tab* key to trigger the autocompletion.

Command predictions

Popularized by the **fish shell**, we can also have PSReadLine show **predictions** based on our history, displayed in a faint text in our prompt. For example, in *Figure 8.8*, we can see that we typed `git` into our prompt, and we have a faint `status` prediction, without needing to trigger autocomplete at all! Pressing the right arrow key would accept the prediction, while continuing to type would refine the prediction. This is separate from the autocompletion modes we covered previously and works well in tandem with them:

Figure 8.8 – PSReadLine predicting we'll type "status" after we type "git"

This can be enabled with the following entry to our PowerShell `$profile`:

```
Set-PSReadLineOption -PredictionSource History
```

To test it out, open a new PowerShell tab in Windows Terminal, type a command such as `ls C:\Windows\System32\`, and press *Enter*. Then, type `ls` again, and PSReadLine will predict the `C:\Windows\System32` path.

Programmable shortcuts

The final command we'll look at is the most flexible; we can associate arbitrary PowerShell code with keyboard shortcuts. For example, if we wanted the *Ctrl + Shift + C* keyboard shortcut to copy the **current working directory** to the clipboard, we could use the following entry in our PowerShell `$profile`:

```
Set-PSReadlineKeyHandler -Key Ctrl+Shift+C `
  -BriefDescription CopyPathToClipboard `
  -LongDescription "Copies the current path to the
    clipboard" `
  -ScriptBlock { (Resolve-Path -LiteralPath
    $pwd).ProviderPath.Trim() | clip }
```

This handler can also access the input buffer of our terminal and modify what we've typed. This makes it possible to program advanced editing and autocompletion behaviors. The `SamplesPSReadLineProfile.ps1` file in the PSReadLine repository contains some interesting example implementations, such as smart parentheses and quote matching. Check it out at `https://github.com/PowerShell/PSReadLine/blob/master/PSReadLine/SamplePSReadLineProfile.ps1`.

We're now done covering the most interesting options available in PSReadLine, but there are many more ways we can use this library, and new features are always being added! Keep up to date with new releases and features by reading the release notes at `https://github.com/PowerShell/PSReadLine/releases`.

Adding the GNU coreutils to the path

Although PowerShell Core has a rich command-line language, it's also nice to have the **GNU coreutils** at our disposal. The GNU coreutils are the typical **Unix** command-line tools such as `ls`, `grep`, `awk`, and `sort`. They are a succinct, popular way of processing data and files, especially on Linux and macOS:

```
~  echo "hello" "howdy" "goodbye" "hola" "hello" | grep ^h | sort | uniq
hello
hola
howdy
```

Figure 8.9 – The GNU coreutils used to process lines of text in PowerShell

The easiest way to install the GNU coreutils is to install Git, which bundles these coreutils. During installation, the installer asks whether you want to **Use Git and optional Unix tools from the Command Prompt**. Selecting that option will make these coreutils available to PowerShell.

> **Note**
>
> The GNU coreutils tools distributed with Git (from the MinGW project) have some issues when dealing with Unicode characters, especially in CJK locales. For quick and dirty processing of mostly Latin/English characters, it's fine; but for other locales, it's better to use WSL2.

If Git is already installed and the coreutils are not available, add the `C:\Program Files\Git\usr\bin` directory to the end of the `Path` system environment variable and restart Windows Terminal.

After the coreutils are installed, we have the option to switch from the PowerShell `ls` tool to the more full-featured coreutils `ls` tool, which provides many more options for displaying and sorting files, yet is terser by default. In *Figure 8.10*, we can see the default, verbose PowerShell `ls` output on the left and the more typical coreutils `ls` output on the right:

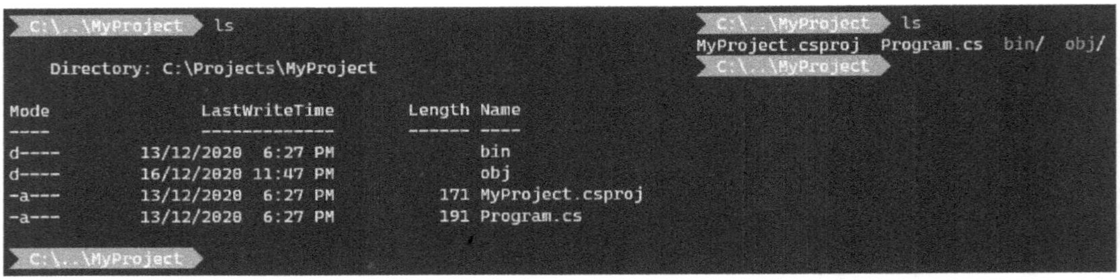

```
C:\..\MyProject  ls                             C:\..\MyProject  ls
                                                MyProject.csproj  Program.cs  bin/  obj/
    Directory: C:\Projects\MyProject            C:\..\MyProject

Mode            LastWriteTime      Length Name
----            -------------      ------ ----
d----      13/12/2020  6:27 PM            bin
d----      16/12/2020 11:47 PM            obj
-a---      13/12/2020  6:27 PM        171 MyProject.csproj
-a---      13/12/2020  6:27 PM        191 Program.cs

C:\..\MyProject
```

Figure 8.10 – Left: the default ls output on PowerShell. Right: the coreutils ls output on PowerShell

This is optional and up to personal taste. To switch from the PowerShell `ls` to the coreutils `ls`, we can put the following PowerShell alias in our `$profile` file:

```
function ls_alias {
  & 'C:\Program Files\Git\usr\bin\ls' --color=auto -hF $args
}
Set-Alias -Name ls -Value ls_alias -Option Private
```

The `-Option Private` flag makes the alias affect only the current scope, limiting the chance that this change will break other scripts. However, it may still break scripts that incorrectly assume that `ls` is an alias to PowerShell's `Get-ChildItem`. If we ever need the original `ls` behavior, we can use the `gci` alias for `Get-ChildItem`.

The GNU coreutils provide a time-tested, popular way of solving problems at the command line; learning and using them with PowerShell is definitely worth it.

Installing the z utility

The final tip we'll cover is the PowerShell z utility. This is a useful, third-party utility that remembers frequently accessed directories and provides a fast way to jump to them, using **Mozilla's frecency algorithm**. (*Frecency* is a mix of frequency and recency.) This is a useful command that essentially lets us jump directly to any previously visited directory without needing to navigate through any of the parent directories on the way to that directory.

For example, say we navigated to the `~/Desktop/MyProject` directory. Sometime later, typing `z MyProj` and pressing *Enter* would automatically navigate back to the `~/Desktop/MyProject` directory, because the text `MyProj` matches a portion of the directory name. If multiple directories are matched, we can press *Tab* to cycle through the matches.

Let's install it into PowerShell Core:

1. Run the `Install-Module z -AllowClobber` command from PowerShell Core. The `-AllowClobber` flag allows it to overwrite the `cd` command with a wrapped version that will keep track of our visited directories.

2. Open the PowerShell `$profile` file and add the line `Import-Module z` to it.

This simple utility can make a surprisingly large difference. Being able to jump to any directory without needing to traverse the filesystem hierarchy first reduces both time and cognitive load.

Addendum – the full PowerShell $profile file

We've covered a lot of commands and settings throughout this chapter, many of which require updating the PowerShell $profile file. Here's a full $profile file that makes use of all these options, all in one place:

```
# only apply to terminals, don't apply to e.g. ISE.
if ($host.Name -eq 'ConsoleHost') {
    Import-Module PSReadLine
    # use vi bindings, but selectively re-enable others
    Set-PSReadLineOption -EditMode Vi
    Set-PSReadLineKeyHandler -Key Ctrl+a -Function
        SelectAll
    Set-PSReadLineKeyHandler -Key Ctrl+c -Function
        CopyOrCancelLine
    Set-PSReadLineKeyHandler -Key Ctrl+x -Function Cut
    Set-PSReadLineKeyHandler -Key Ctrl+v -Function Paste
    Set-PSReadLineKeyHandler -Key Shift+LeftArrow -Function
        SelectBackwardChar
    Set-PSReadLineKeyHandler -Key Shift+RightArrow
        -Function SelectForwardChar
    Set-PSReadLineKeyHandler -Key Ctrl+Shift+LeftArrow
        -Function SelectBackwardWord
    Set-PSReadLineKeyHandler -Key Ctrl+Shift+RightArrow
        -Function SelectNextWord

    Set-PSReadLineOption -PredictionSource History
    Set-PSReadLineOption -HistorySearchCursorMovesToEnd
    Set-PSReadLineKeyHandler -Key Tab -Function
        MenuComplete
    Set-PSReadLineKeyHandler -Key UpArrow -Function
        HistorySearchBackward
    Set-PSReadLineKeyHandler -Key DownArrow -Function
        HistorySearchForward
    Set-PSReadlineOption -BellStyle None
    Set-PSReadlineKeyHandler -Key Ctrl+Shift+C `
            -BriefDescription CopyPathToClipboard `
            -LongDescription "Copies the current path to the
                clipboard" `
            -ScriptBlock { (Resolve-Path -LiteralPath
                $pwd).ProviderPath.Trim() | clip }
    # Make the "Command Predictions" a little more obvious
```

```
Set-PSReadlineOption -Color @{
    "InlinePrediction" = [ConsoleColor]::DarkCyan
}
Import-Module oh-my-posh
Set-PoshPrompt
# jump to frequently used directories with z
Import-Module z
# use the coreutils ls instead of Get-ChildItem
function ls_alias { & 'C:\Program Files\Git\usr\bin\ls'
  --color=auto -hF $args }
Set-Alias -Name ls -Value ls_alias -Option Private
}
```

Summary

In this chapter, we learned how to use the basic PowerShell Core command line to the fullest, using useful variables such as $$ and $^, and commands such as cd -, cd +, ii, h, and r. We also learned about PowerShell functions and pipelines.

After that, we turbocharged our editing experience with PSReadLine and created a full-featured, programmable PowerShell prompt. Luckily, there's very little we need to program ourselves—we can make use of the existing modules and configurations available from the community.

Additionally, we learned how to access coreutils from our PowerShell prompt. This gives us access to a large, popular suite of command-line tools that excel at manipulating text and solving problems.

Finally, we installed the z utility, which allows us to navigate around the filesystem at warp speed.

Now that we can run PowerShell like a pro, let's jump into the next chapter, where we will do the same for Linux on WSL2.

9
Tips for Using Ubuntu like an Expert

In this chapter, we'll amp up our power at the command line by using **Ubuntu** inside the **Windows Subsystem for Linux 2 (WSL2)**. There are two main areas we'll cover: using WSL2 features to break down the barrier between Windows and Linux, and using the Linux shell to issue commands at warp speed.

The Linux command line sets the standard for high productivity in command-line systems. Often, command-line enhancements and inventions are initially available on Linux, and eventually make their way to Windows. Many of the tips we learned in the previous chapter for PowerShell were cloned from their Linux counterparts; we'll cover these counterparts in this chapter so we have a consistent command-line experience across both operating systems.

Technical requirements

This chapter assumes that a Linux distribution is installed inside WSL2, as covered in *Chapter 3, Configuring an Ubuntu Linux Profile*, and that **ZSH** is installed, as covered in *Chapter 5, Changing your Windows Terminal appearance*, in the *WSL2 customization with oh-my-zsh* section. We'll be using **Ubuntu 20.04** in this chapter, but the majority of tips apply to any Linux distribution. The configuration options we discuss in this chapter are available online at `https://github.com/PacktPublishing/Windows-Terminal-Tips-Tricks/tree/main/Chapter 09`.

Using Ubuntu with Windows

WSL2 is technically a lightweight **virtual machine**. While virtual machines are historically partitioned off from their host operating system, WSL2 provides some useful ways to transfer both data and commands across that boundary, making it easier and faster to accomplish our goals by combining the strengths of Windows and Linux.

Accessing Linux directories from Windows

From time to time, we'll want to transfer files from our Windows system to our Linux system. For example, maybe we have a large text file we want to ingest into a Linux command-line tool for further processing.

WSL2 creates a locally restricted **network share** for each installed distribution, under the `\\wsl$` prefix. For example, our Ubuntu filesystem root is available under the `\\wsl$\Ubuntu\` network path:

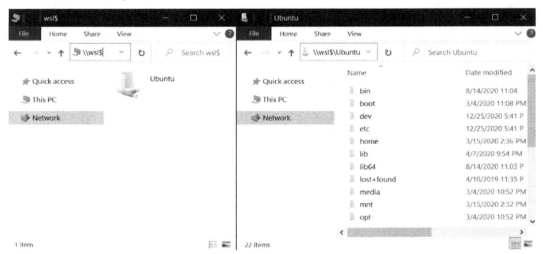

Figure 9.1 – WSL2 creates a network share that exposes our Linux filesystems to Windows

Using Windows Explorer, we can move, copy, and edit our Linux files using Windows applications. Unlike earlier versions of WSL, WSL2 has improved filesystem performance, and will not corrupt the files when editing.

Microsoft recommends that for the best performance, we should use Linux applications to edit Linux files, and Windows applications to edit Windows files. In a pinch, however, we can still take advantage of this interoperability to transfer files across operating systems.

Accessing Windows directories from Linux

We can also go in the other direction, and open Windows files from inside Linux. All our drives are automatically mounted inside the /mnt/ directory of the Linux filesystem. For example, our C: drive can be found under /mnt/c/:

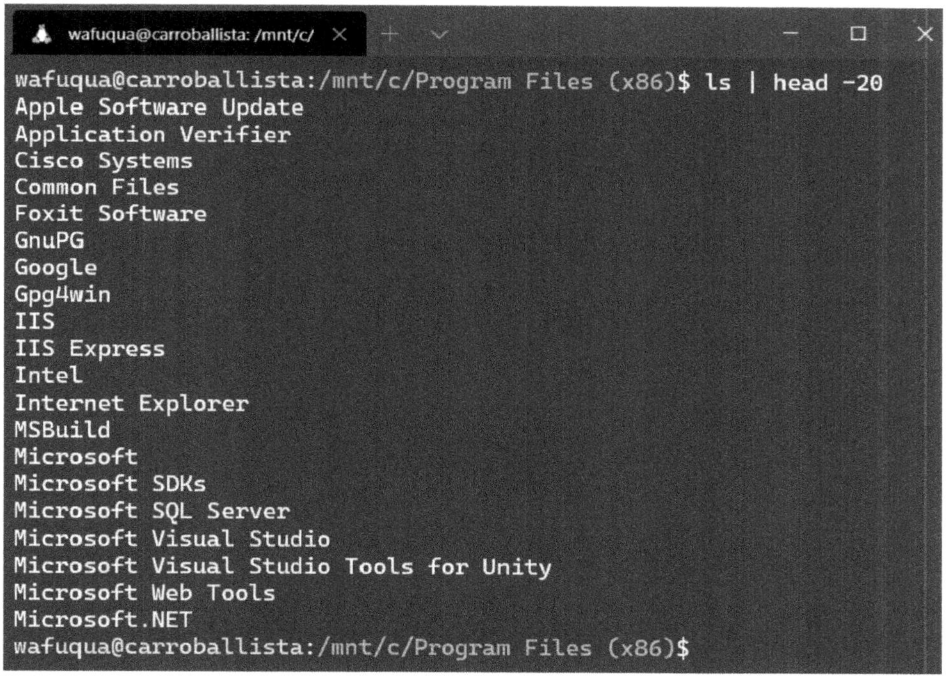

```
wafuqua@carroballista: /mnt/c/  ×

wafuqua@carroballista:/mnt/c/Program Files (x86)$ ls | head -20
Apple Software Update
Application Verifier
Cisco Systems
Common Files
Foxit Software
GnuPG
Google
Gpg4win
IIS
IIS Express
Intel
Internet Explorer
MSBuild
Microsoft
Microsoft SDKs
Microsoft SQL Server
Microsoft Visual Studio
Microsoft Visual Studio Tools for Unity
Microsoft Web Tools
Microsoft.NET
wafuqua@carroballista:/mnt/c/Program Files (x86)$
```

Figure 9.2 – Accessing the Windows C: drive from Linux

As expected, we can use editors and command-line tools to manipulate our Windows files. We'll be subject to Windows permissions; we can't automatically write to /mnt/c/ Windows, for example, unless the Windows 10 permissions are set up to allow it.

Running Linux programs from inside Windows

We're not restricted to just moving and editing files; we can also run Linux applications and commands from inside PowerShell or Command Prompt! WSL2 provides the **wsl.exe** command-line utility, which can execute commands inside Linux and return the results to our Windows command line. We can seamlessly pipe command output and files to Linux command-line utilities.

For example, let's run a PowerShell command, and then send the output from that command, or *pipe* it, to be processed by a Linux command. We'll use `Get-ChildItem` as our PowerShell command, which can list files in the current directory, and `grep` as our Linux command, which can search text for keywords. The following command will search for the word `hello` in the filenames of all hidden files in the current directory:

```
Get-ChildItem -Hidden | wsl grep hello
```

This will run the `Get-ChildItem -Hidden` PowerShell command to show hidden files in the current Windows directory, and then pipe it to `wsl.exe`, where the `grep` utility will search the output for the `hello` substring.

> **Note**
>
> Throughout this section, we'll use the term *Linux utilities* as a shorthand for *Utilities available on the Linux command line*. However, many of the utilities we'll use in our examples are actually part of the **GNU coreutils** project, not the Linux project.

Additionally, we can seamlessly pass Windows files to Linux utilities. For example, from PowerShell, we can use the `wc` command from inside WSL2 to count the number of lines in a Windows file:

```
wsl wc -l desktop.ini
```

This command will run the `wc` utility from Ubuntu on our Windows file, `MyFile.txt`, and return the output to our PowerShell window. This is demonstrated in the following screenshot:

Figure 9.3 – PowerShell commands and Linux commands can be combined freely

This shows that we don't need to treat WSL2 as a completely separate system; we can use the `wsl` command to chain together Windows utilities and Linux utilities at the command line.

Astute readers may be wondering why we would use the `wsl.exe` utility, given that we installed the GNU coreutils natively on Windows 10 in the previous chapter. Each implementation has its own benefits.

The benefits of the `wsl.exe` utility is that it can run any Linux command-line application, not just the coreutils. Additionally, for the coreutils, the `wsl.exe` utility is running the more popular Linux implementations of the GNU coreutils, so there's a higher chance that any documentation and examples we find will work.

The benefits of the native GNU coreutils is that they don't require prefixing every invocation with the `wsl` command. Additionally, they tend to have better compatibility with Windows filenames, path separators, and other Windows peculiarities. Finally, the native GNU coreutils are slightly faster than running through WSL2; however, the difference won't be noticeable the vast majority of the time.

Running Windows programs from inside Linux

Just like we can call Linux utilities from Windows, we can also call Windows programs from Linux. WSL2 supports invoking arbitrary Windows programs, as long as they end in the `.exe` file extension. For example, if we wanted to use **Windows Notepad** to edit a file in Ubuntu, we could type `notepad.exe filename`, as seen in the following screenshot:

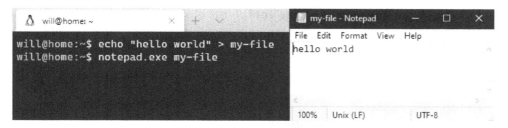

Figure 9.4 – Starting notepad.exe, a Windows application, from inside Ubuntu

Similarly, if we wanted to open **Windows Explorer** in the current Linux directory, we could type `explorer.exe .`, where `.` represents the current directory:

Figure 9.5 – Using Windows Explorer to access a Linux directory in the WSL2 network share

Another useful trick is to use Windows' `clip.exe` utility to write to the Windows clipboard from Linux applications. Simply piping text to `clip.exe` will automatically put it on the Windows clipboard. This can be a useful way to integrate more complex command-line applications running in Linux (such as **Vim** or **Emacs**), with Windows 10.

Installing and configuring software

Ubuntu, like most other Linux distributions, has a vast array of high-quality software available in its **package repositories**. In Ubuntu, we can easily install this software using the **APT** command-line utility.

APT (which stands for **Advanced Package Tool**) is the most popular and well-supported way of installing software in Ubuntu. For example, we can use it to find and install `nmap`, an open source network mapping and security tool:

1. Find the package name by updating our list of packages, and then searching them:

    ```
    sudo apt update
    apt search "network mapper"
    ```

    This returns a package name of `nmap`.

2. Install the package with the following command:

    ```
    sudo apt install nmap
    ```

3. We can keep all system software and applications up to date by running the following two commands periodically:

```
sudo apt update
sudo apt upgrade
```

4. After nmap is installed, we can map our local network with a command like the following:

```
sudo nmap -sS 192.168.1.*
```

This prints a list of every host on our local network from `192.168.1.1` to `192.168.1.255`, along with any open ports.

Note that this command should only be run on networks we own, such as a home network, rather than a corporate network. The corporate network administrator might not be happy if we scan every host on the network!

Choosing your shell

One of the biggest productivity enhancements we can make to our Ubuntu installation is changing the default **shell**. Ubuntu comes with the **Bash shell** by default, which is speedy and perfectly usable. We can increase our productivity, however, by choosing either the **Z shell** (**ZSH**) or **fish shell**. Both of these shells provide better out-of-the-box experiences than Bash.

ZSH is one of the most popular shells on Linux, and is the default shell on macOS since Catalina. It has 30 years of history, is highly configurable, and has a strong community with a large set of community-created themes and customizations. We first learned about ZSH in *Chapter 5, Changing your Windows Terminal appearance*, where we used the **oh-my-zsh** project to modernize our terminal's look. That just barely scratched the surface of the configurability and flexibility of ZSH; we'll learn more about it in the following sections.

Also worth mentioning is the fish shell; this shell has grown very popular recently due to its high rate of innovation and user-centric design. Unlike ZSH, fish breaks compatibility with older shells and standards, so there can be compatibility issues with older, more complex scripts, but this allows the fish shell to experiment in ways that other shells cannot. We won't be covering the fish shell in this book, but more information can be found at `https://fishshell.com/`:

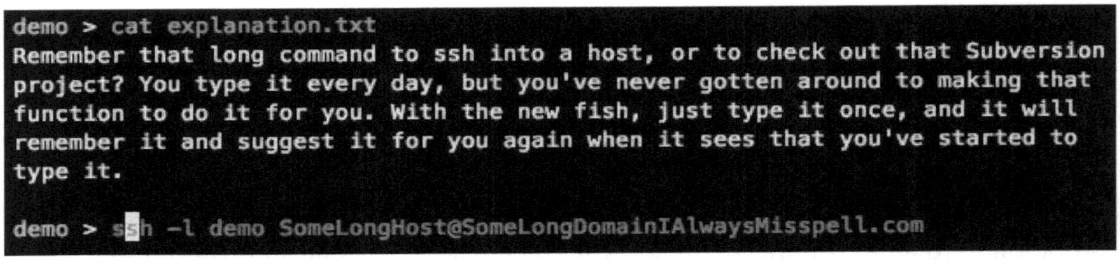

```
demo > cat explanation.txt
Remember that long command to ssh into a host, or to check out that Subversion
project? You type it every day, but you've never gotten around to making that
function to do it for you. With the new fish, just type it once, and it will
remember it and suggest it for you again when it sees that you've started to
type it.

demo > ssh -l demo SomeLongHost@SomeLongDomainIAlwaysMisspell.com
```

Figure 9.6 – The fish shell, as shown from fishshell.com

As we already covered the installation and configuration of ZSH in *Chapter 5, Changing your Windows Terminal appearance*, we won't cover it again here. We can verify whether ZSH is set up correctly by running `echo $SHELL`. If it returns `/bin/zsh` or `/usr/bin/zsh` then we're good to go; if not, follow the steps in *Chapter 5, Changing your Windows Terminal appearance*, to set up ZSH correctly.

Using ZSH

To make configuration a little easier, we'll be using oh-my-zsh to configure much of our ZSH experience. It's worth keeping in mind, however, that everything we do in this section is possible without oh-my-zsh; oh-my-zsh simply provides bundles of ZSH configurations with reasonable defaults. The real workhorse is ZSH!

For example, ZSH provides a useful `up-line-or-beginning-search` option, which is often left unused. If we enable this option, when we type some text at the prompt and press the up arrow, ZSH will search through our history for the typed text. Installing oh-my-zsh will automatically enable this option.

Let's walk through some of the options available in ZSH. After that, we'll discuss what oh-my-zsh adds on top of ZSH, both out of the box and via plugins.

Rerunning earlier commands

Like PowerShell, ZSH provides multiple ways to rerun earlier commands, so we don't need to retype them or press the up arrow repeatedly to find some earlier command.

The first way we'll cover is the *Ctrl + R* keyboard shortcut, which is the same shortcut we used in **PSReadLine** in the previous chapter. By pressing *Ctrl + R*, ZSH enters **search mode**, where we can search for our previously issued commands. Pressing *Enter* will select a command to run:

Figure 9.7 – Using Ctrl + R to search for "log" returns the "git log --pretty=oneline" command

Another way we can run an earlier command is by typing an exclamation mark, and then the prefix of the command we want to run. Pressing *Enter* will select the command to run, while pressing *Tab* will autocomplete the command inline in our current prompt:

Figure 9.8 – Using the exclamation mark (!) to quickly re-run previous commands by their prefixes

Like PSReadLine from the previous chapter, we can also enable inline predictions based on historical commands; we'll cover how to do that later in our section on oh-my-zsh plugins.

Using ZSH substitutions

Similar to PowerShell, we also have **history substitutions** for referring to parts of the previous command. The substitution names are prefixed with an exclamation point, rather than the dollar sign that PowerShell uses. When ZSH detects these symbols in a command, it will substitute them with a portion of the previously executed command:

- !$ is replaced with the last argument of the previous command. For example, we could use it to edit a file we just renamed:

```
mv old.json new.json
vim !$
```

In this case, ZSH would turn `vim !$` into `vim new.json`.

- `!^` is replaced with the first argument of the previous command.
- `!*` is replaced with all arguments of the previous command. This can be useful if we copied a file, then realized we wanted to move it instead:

```
cp old.json new.json
mv !*
```

In this case, ZSH would turn `mv !*` into `mv old.json new.json`.

- `!:n` is replaced with the nth argument of the previous command, where n is an integer.
- `!!` is replaced with the entire previous command.

This final `!!` substitution, which represents the entire previous command, is especially useful if we run a command that requires **sudo** (that is, **root**) privileges, but forget to prefix the command with `sudo`. Running `sudo !!` will prepopulate our prompt with the previous command, including the required `sudo` prefix. Additionally, pressing *Tab* after typing `!!` will automatically expand the substitution:

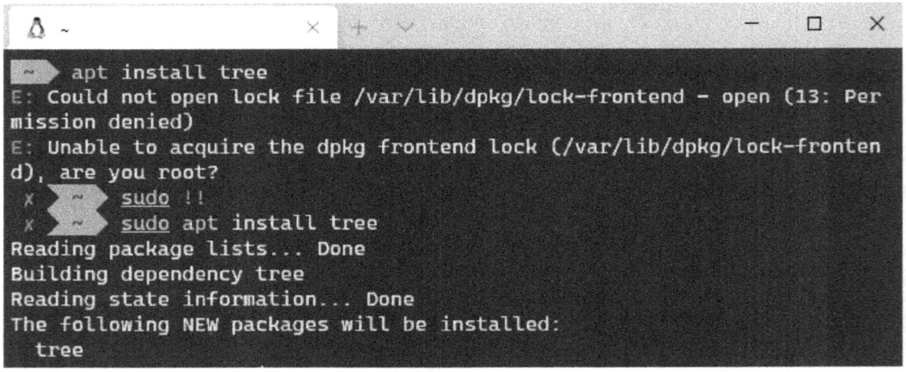

Figure 9.9 – Using !! to prefix a previous command with "sudo"

By using these ZSH history substitutions, we can rapidly iterate on commands, without needing to retype lengthy commands and file paths.

Configuring aliases and functions

Again like PowerShell, we can define aliases at the command line to provide shortcuts for commonly executed commands. The combination of this, along with the interoperability possibilities we covered in the first section of this chapter, unlocks a large potential for workflow improvements!

To demonstrate, let's recreate the useful `ii` alias from PowerShell, but in Linux. This alias opens the supplied file in the *Default Application* as specified in the Windows 10 settings:

```
alias ii="powershell.exe -Command invoke-item"
```

We can type this alias into our shell, and then use this new `ii` alias to open text files, HTML files, images, or even directories:

Figure 9.10 – Calling PowerShell's Invoke-Item command from Linux, using a ZSH alias

Because we entered this alias into our shell, it is currently a *temporary alias*, which will not persist in future instances of ZSH. If we want this alias to become a *permanent alias*, we can put it at the end of our `~/.zshrc` file. This is a hidden file that controls the configuration of ZSH.

While we could use this alias to shorten the name of our favorite editor, as we did in the previous chapter on PowerShell, ZSH provides a more powerful type of alias to handle this scenario: **suffix aliases**.

Suffix aliases allow us to associate an application, like an editor or viewer, with a file extension. When we evaluate a file with the specified extension (that is, typing just the filename and pressing *Enter*), the specified application will automatically run.

For example, if we wanted to open all JSON files with the Vim editor, we could set the following alias. Note that it uses an `-s` switch to indicate it's a suffix alias:

```
alias -s json=vim
```

Now, when we type `test.json` at the command line, it will open in our editor, without needing to type the editor's name at all! See the following screenshot:

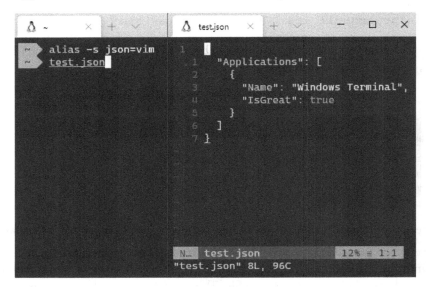

Figure 9.11 – Using suffix aliases to open JSON files in a default editor

We can set all sorts of suffix aliases for handling images, text files, source code, and archives. Because we learned how to invoke Windows executables from Linux earlier, we could even set up a suffix alias that points to a Windows executable!

Another nice trick is to set up suffix aliases for archives, such as `.zip` files and `.tar` files, with Vim. This allows us to browse and edit archives interactively with the Vim editor:

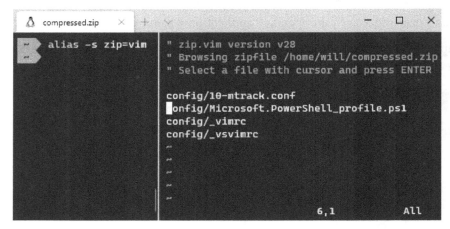

Figure 9.12 – Configuring archives to open with the Vim editor – the compressed files can be edited in place

ZSH also supports **functions**, for when we want to create aliases that can't be represented as a simple string replacement. For example, let's recreate our `work` function from the previous PowerShell chapter. As a refresher, it navigated to a specific directory, opened Visual Studio Code, and refreshed the status of all Git remotes. In ZSH, the function would look like this:

```
work() {
  cd ~/projects/my-project
  code .
  git fetch --all
}
```

> **Note**
>
> For the `code` command to work in WSL2, make sure the `Remote - WSL` extension is installed in Visual Studio Code, running in Windows 10.

Now, typing `work` at the command line will execute all three commands. If we didn't want to hardcode this function to the `~/projects/my-project` directory, we can use the `$1` variable to refer to the first function argument (and `$2` for the second argument, and so on):

```
work() {
  cd $1
  code .
  git fetch --all
}
```

Now, typing `work ~/some/other/project` would navigate to the `~/some/other/project` directory, open Visual Studio Code, and refresh the status of all Git remotes!

Quickly navigating to directories

A surprisingly large amount of shell usage involves navigating back and forth between directories. ZSH has several features that allow us to do this efficiently, with minimal keypresses.

Just like we can use suffix aliases to evaluate files at the command line and it *does the right thing*, we can also evaluate directories to automatically navigate to them:

Figure 9.13 – Using autocd to navigate without the "cd" command

This requires us to enable the `autocd` configuration option, by putting the `setopt autocd` line in our `.zshrc` configuration file. Alternatively, if oh-my-zsh is installed, this option is set automatically.

We can switch back and forth between the two most recent directories by typing - (*hyphen*):

Figure 9.14 – Using "-" to toggle between the two most recent directories

By typing - repeatedly, we toggled between the home directory (~) and the `projects` directory. We never went back to the `demo` directory because the - command only switches between the two most recent directories.

If we wanted to go back to the `demo` directory, we could make use of another ZSH feature, the `autopushd` configuration option. By putting the `setopt autopushd` line in our `.zshrc` configuration file (or by using oh-my-zsh, which enables it automatically), ZSH will automatically keep track of the directories we navigate to. ZSH uses a **stack** data structure, and will automatically *push* directories onto this stack as we navigate to them. We can then *pop* directories from this stack with the `popd` command:

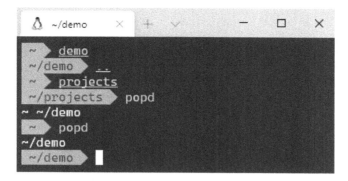

Figure 9.15 – Using autopushd and popd to navigate back through our history of directories

So far, we've been covering tips and tricks for using ZSH's built-in functionality effectively. Now, let's switch gears and discuss extending ZSH with oh-my-zsh plugins.

Installing and using oh-my-zsh plugins

Oh-my-zsh has a large collection of **plugins**. These plugins generally cover the following three areas, but are not restricted to them:

- **Plugins that add aliases**: For example, the **Ruby** plugin for oh-my-zsh provides aliases such as `gin`, which expands to `gem install`.

- **Plugins that add autocompletion support for specific applications**: For example, the **Rust** plugin adds autocompletion for the `rustc` compiler command-line parameters.

- **Plugins that modify how the command line works**: For example, the **zsh-syntax-highlighting** plugin adds syntax highlighting for the command-line input (such as strings, command-line parameters, comments, and so on).

Oh-my-zsh has over 250 plugins available and documented on GitHub (`https://github.com/ohmyzsh/ohmyzsh/wiki/Plugins`). Plugins can greatly enhance our productivity, but be careful; installing too many plugins, or poorly written plugins, can decrease the overall performance of ZSH. In this chapter, we'll recommend four plugins to get started, and cover how to install and use each of them.

Enabling the z plugin

We first learned about the **z** plugin in the previous chapter, when we enabled it for PowerShell. It remembers frequently accessed directories, and allows us to jump to these directories by providing a substring of the directory path. We can jump directly to any previously visited directory, without needing to navigate through any of the parent directories on the way to that directory:

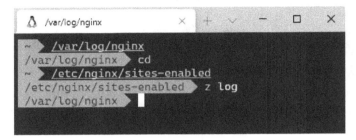

Figure 9.16 – Using z to quickly jump to frequently/recently used directories

The z plugin is built into oh-my-zsh, so we can enable it without installing any further software:

1. Open the .zshrc file and find the line starting with plugins= (as shown in *Figure 9.17*) This line represents the list of enabled plugins in oh-my-zsh.

2. Add the z plugin to this line. Plugins are separated by spaces, not commas!

3. Save the file.

4. Reload ZSH by running source .zshrc from the home directory:

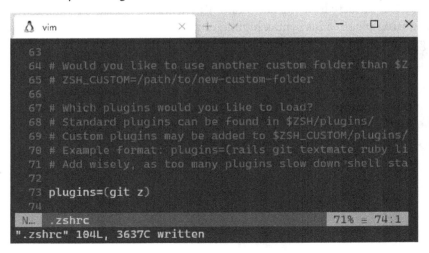

Figure 9.17 – Enabling the z plugin in our .zshrc file

All the oh-my-zsh plugins that we'll cover in the remainder of this chapter will be enabled this way.

Enabling vi-mode

For those who use Vim, enabling **vi-mode** in oh-my-zsh provides familiar key bindings for effortlessly manipulating text. This oh-my-zsh plugin simply wraps the vi-mode provided by ZSH itself, and provides a little bit of extra configuration for areas such as visual mode emulation and other keyboard shortcuts.

vi-mode is also built into oh-my-zsh, so we can enable it with the same steps as the previous plugin: find the plugins line in the .zshrc file, add vi-mode to the list, and reload ZSH.

Installing zsh-autosuggestions

The **zsh-autosuggestions** plugin can automatically provide suggestions for commands based on our history. This is similar to the PowerShell prediction functionality that we enabled in the previous chapter.

In this mode, ZSH will display the suggestion in a faint text in our current prompt, as seen in the following screenshot. Pressing the right arrow key will accept the autosuggestion, and continuing to type will further refine the suggestion:

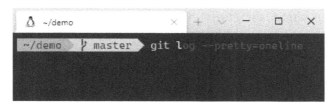

Figure 9.18 – A subtle suggestion for a longer git log command, provided by zsh-autosuggestions

Unlike our previous plugins, this plugin is not part of oh-my-zsh and will need to be installed separately. Luckily, all it takes is cloning a Git repo! Simply clone the Git repository at https://github.com/zsh-users/zsh-autosuggestions into the ~/.oh-my-zsh/custom/plugins directory.

After that, add zsh-autosuggestions to the plugins in the .zshrc file, and reload ZSH. After a few commands have been issued, suggestions will begin to appear in the prompt.

zsh-syntax-highlighting

The final plugin we'll look at is **zsh-syntax-highlighting**. This plugin will apply syntax highlighting to our input prompt. For example, it highlights the primary command in green to make it stand out, as well as any strings and variables in the command-line arguments:

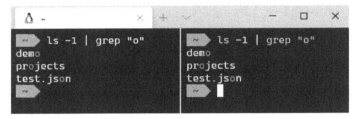

Figure 9.19 – Left: commands without syntax highlighting; right: commands with syntax highlighting

`zsh-syntax-highlighting` provides the following readability benefits:

- Long, chained commands are easier to read because each part of the command is highlighted.
- Missing closing quotes are easier to identify due to the string syntax coloring.
- Parentheses and brackets are easier to match up because each matching pair is colored differently. This is optional and is disabled by default.

Similar to the previous plugin, the `zsh-syntax-highlighting` plugin can be installed by cloning the Git repo at `https://github.com/zsh-users/zsh-syntax-highlighting` into the `.oh-my-zsh/custom/plugins` directory, and then enabling it in the `.zshrc` plugins as we did in previous sections.

When adding `zsh-syntax-highlighting` to the `plugins` array, make sure to append it to the very end. Plugins are executed sequentially according to their order in this array, and this plugin needs the final state of the prompt in order to determine the correct colors:

```
plugins=(git z zsh-autosuggestions zsh-syntax-highlighting)
```

The `zsh-syntax-highlighting` plugin has several optional highlighters; by default only the `main` highlighter is enabled. To enable parentheses and bracket highlighting, we can set the following line in our `.zshrc`, before the `oh-my-zsh.sh` script is run:

```
ZSH_HIGHLIGHT_HIGHLIGHTERS=(main brackets)
```

There are other highlighter options beyond just `main` and `brackets`; check out the `highlighters.md` file available at `https://github.com/zsh-users/zsh-syntax-highlighting/blob/master/docs/highlighters.md` for a full list.

Summary

We started this chapter with an overview of how to bridge the gap between Windows and Linux with WSL2's interoperability features. This allows us to seamlessly share both files and commands between these two operating systems.

We then reviewed how to install and update software in Ubuntu, so we can greatly increase the amount of software at our fingertips. With both the Windows 10 platform and the Ubuntu package repository available to us, we'll be able to install almost any piece of software available!

Then, we discussed the concept of alternate shells, and selected ZSH to replace our default shell. We learned how to use ZSH effectively with command substitutions, aliases, suffix aliases, and functions. Finally, we covered using oh-my-zsh's plugins to add useful features including autosuggestions, syntax highlighting, and more.

In our next few chapters, we'll focus on optimizing common developer and DevOps workflows so we can move quickly and effortlessly at the command line. First up: optimizing our Git and GitHub usage!

Section 3: Using your Windows Terminal for development

In this section, we'll cover how to effectively perform common development and operational tasks with our Windows Terminal. We'll show common patterns in frontend development, backend development, remote machine connections, and cloud management, using Windows Terminal throughout.

This section comprises the following chapters:

- *Chapter 10, Using Git and GitHub with Windows Terminal*
- *Chapter 11, Building web applications with React*
- *Chapter 12, Building REST APIs with C# and Windows Terminal*
- *Chapter 13, Connecting to remote systems*
- *Chapter 14, Managing systems in the cloud*

10
Using Git and GitHub with Windows Terminal

Throughout this book, we've been using a great deal of open source software, such as Windows Terminal, PowerShell, and ZSH. These three projects all have something in common: they use Git as their **version control system** (**VCS**) to manage their source code.

Git is the most popular version control system, as it's fast, flexible, and **distributed**. Its distributed nature is in contrast to older *client/server* systems such as **Subversion** (**SVN**), where the server has all the smarts, and the clients are dependent on it. With Git, each copy of the source code is a fully working repository with a complete history of the code, and can itself act as a server if required. Whether or not there's a central copy in Git is more of a social or project management construct, rather than a technical one.

Somewhat ironically, one of the most popular ways to use Git is in a centralized manner, with **GitHub** and **GitLab** being the common hosts. In this chapter, we'll explore how to use Git and GitHub in Windows Terminal, and get a consistent, low-friction experience across both Windows and Linux. In addition, we'll cover a few tips and tricks for speeding up common Git operations.

We'll cover the following topics:

- Creating a modern Git installation
- Tips for using Git effectively
- Using GitHub from Windows Terminal

Technical requirements

In this chapter, we'll be using the version of **OpenSSH** that comes bundled with Windows 10. We'll require at least **Windows 10 Version 1809** (released in November 2018).

Additionally, it's assumed that posh-git, a PowerShell module that integrates Git and PowerShell, is already installed as covered in *Chapter 8, Tips for Using PowerShell like a Pro*.

As always, the materials for this chapter are available online at
`https://github.com/PacktPublishing/Windows-Terminal-Tips-Tricks/tree/main/Chapter 10`.

Creating a modern Git installation

In this section, we'll configure Git in Windows 10 in a modern and secure way. In the past, Git didn't always run well on Windows 10; several third-party utilities were required to get everything working, and we often had to re-enter our password. That's changed since late 2018; now we can get a first class Git experience on Windows 10.

When using Git, and especially GitHub, we need to decide between **HTTPS authentication** versus **SSH authentication**. HTTPS authentication is easier to get started with, but SSH authentication has some workflow benefits. In this book, we will use SSH authentication, for the following reasons:

- It leads to a more streamlined workflow when combined with **ssh-agent**.
- It allows our workflow to be very similar between Windows 10, WSL2, and even macOS.
- HTTPS authentication uses the **Windows Credential Manager**. If we need to use SSH to connect to remote hosts, it's nice to manage all authentication in one place, rather than splitting accounts between SSH and the Windows Credential Manager.

Let's begin by installing Git.

Installing Git

To install Git, download and run the installer from `https://git-scm.com/` `download/win`. The Git for Windows installer has a surprising number of options; most can be left at the default value or changed according to personal preference, but the most important options are as follows:

- **Use Git and optional Unix tools from the Command Prompt**. As we covered in *Chapter 8, Tips for Using PowerShell like a Pro*, this allows us to use **GNU Coreutils** from Windows Terminal

- **Use OpenSSH**. We'll use an open source library called **OpenSSH**, which is bundled with recent versions of Windows 10, rather than older **Putty/Pageant**-based workflows.

- Optionally, do **not** enable **Git Bash**, as we're using Windows Terminal instead:

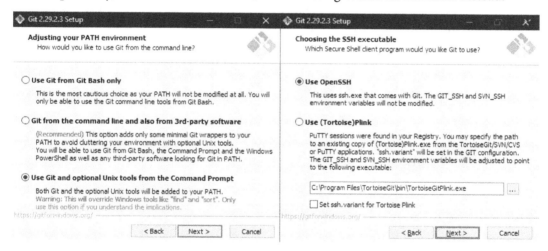

Figure 10.1 – Important settings in the Git for Windows installer

Once Git has been installed successfully, configure the name and email by issuing the following two commands. For activity on GitHub, the email is used to associate commits with the correct GitHub account:

```
git config --global user.name "Joe Smith"
git config --global user.email "joe@example.com"
```

This command will set global configuration options—they'll apply to all Git repositories on our computer.

> **Note**
>
> On GitHub, any public commits are web browsable, which means the email configured here will become publicly visible, potentially to spammers. To help obscure it, GitHub can autogenerate a no-reply email address at `https://github.com/settings/emails`. Use this autogenerated email in the previous `user.email` command.

In the next few sections, we will walk through setting up SSH authentication, and configuring Git to use this SSH authentication. By making our SSH authentication process smooth and streamlined, it will make our Git experience better, too.

Installing OpenSSH

Now that we've set up Git, let's set up OpenSSH. Enable it in Windows 10 by searching for `Optional Features` in the Windows **Start** Menu. If OpenSSH is not already installed, click **Add a feature** and add the **OpenSSH Client** feature, as shown in *Figure 10.2*:

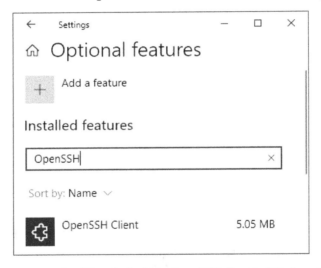

Figure 10.2 – Enabling the built-in OpenSSH client in Windows 10

This will install OpenSSH in `C:\Windows\System32\OpenSSH`. It contains all of the typical OpenSSH tools, including **ssh**, **scp**, and **ssh-agent**.

Now, we can tell Git to use the native OpenSSH installation by setting the `GIT_SSH` environment variable to `C:\Windows\System32\OpenSSH\ssh.exe`. Either set it via the **Environment Variable** editor in Windows 10, or set it from Windows Terminal (running as an administrator) with the following command:

```
setx /M GIT_SSH C:\Windows\System32\OpenSSH\ssh.exe
```

After setting this environment variable, restart Windows Terminal to make sure it gets a fresh copy of all the environment variables.

Starting our OpenSSH Agent

Now that OpenSSH is enabled, let's make sure that the **OpenSSH Authentication Agent** Windows Service is running and set to start automatically. This background service keeps track of our authentication keys, and is responsible for proving to remote servers, like GitHub, that we are who we say we are:

1. Open the **Services** application by searching for `Windows Services` in the **Start** menu.

2. Once the application opens, find **OpenSSH Authentication Agent** in the **Windows Services** application.

3. Make sure that **Status** is **Running**, and that **Startup Type** is **Automatic**, as shown in *Figure 10.3*:

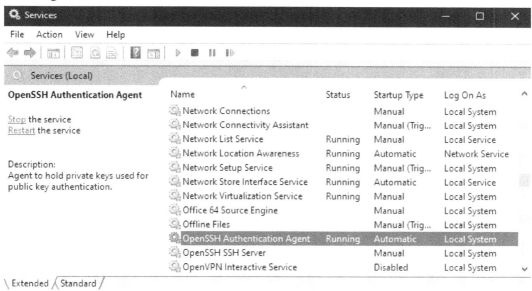

Figure 10.3 – Configuring the OpenSSH Authentication Agent service to start automatically

Watch out for **OpenSSH SSH Server**—although it's similarly named, we don't want to start that! **OpenSSH Authentication Agent** is the one we want.

Setting up a private/public key pair

Now, let's set up our OpenSSH keys. We will generate a single key pair, which consists of two keys: the **public key** and the **private key**. We'll share our public key with GitHub and other users, while keeping our private key a secret. The private key should never be shared with any person or organization, and will never even leave our computer! The public key is safe to share.

Public and private keys can be generated with different cryptographic algorithms. Presently, **ED25519** is the recommended algorithm to use. **RSA**, with its 4096-bit key, is also acceptable. However, ED25519 is shorter, faster, more modern, and, more importantly, more compatible with Windows 10.

If we already have ED25519 private/public keys, we can simply copy them to the C:\ Users\USERNAME\.ssh directory, creating the directory if it doesn't exist.

If we don't have ED25519 keys, we can generate a new key pair now. Open PowerShell, navigate to C:\Users\USERNAME\.ssh, and run the following command:

```
ssh-keygen -t ed25519 -C "some name"
```

In this command, "some name" is a string that identifies the key. For example, this could be the email address associated with the Git account. Set a strong passphrase to protect this key. This will generate two files, a public key named id_ed25519.pub, and a private key named id_ed25519. Remember, never share the private key!

To use GitHub, add the public key to the account page available at https://github. com/settings/keys. To use Git repositories other than GitHub, follow their documented way of sharing the public key.

Add the private key to the SSH agent by running the following command, and then entering the key's passphrase when prompted:

```
ssh-add .\id_ed25519
```

Done! Now let's test it out and make sure it works.

Testing our SSH authentication

To test out our SSH authentication, close Windows Terminal, and then open it again to ensure we have the latest environment variables. Run the command ssh git@ github.com and make sure a You've successfully authenticated message is displayed, as seen in *Figure 10.4*:

```
C:\...\will.fuqua\.ssh                                                    ─  □  ✕
~\.ssh  ls
id_ed25519   id_ed25519.pub
~\.ssh  ssh-add .\id_ed25519
Enter passphrase for .\id_ed25519:
Identity added: .\id_ed25519 (will@example.com)
~\.ssh  ssh git@github.com
The authenticity of host 'github.com (13.236.229.21)' can't be established.
RSA key fingerprint is SHA256:nThbg6kXUpJWGl7E1IGOCspRomTxdCARLviKw6E5SY8.
Are you sure you want to continue connecting (yes/no)? yes
Warning: Permanently added 'github.com,13.236.229.21' (RSA) to the list of known hosts.
PTY allocation request failed on channel 0
Hi will! You've successfully authenticated, but GitHub does not provide shell access.
Connection to github.com closed.
~\.ssh  ▮
```

Figure 10.4 – Testing SSH authentication to GitHub

We didn't need to type in our password when connecting to GitHub. This is because GitHub knows our public key, and our ssh-agent properly used the private key to prove our identity. Even if we restart Windows Terminal, our ssh-agent is still running as a background service, so we don't need to type in our password again.

In the future, when we use Git, it will use SSH, due to our GIT_SSH environment variable. We've set up SSH to authenticate automatically, so Git will authenticate automatically, too. In summary, both Git and SSH are using the same authentication system, and the ssh-agent built into Windows 10 manages it for us.

Authenticating with Git on Linux

Now that we have streamlined SSH-based authentication set up on Windows, let's set the same thing up on our WSL2 Linux! For those that don't plan on using Git on WSL2, proceed to the next section, *Tips for using Git effectively*.

The first thing to decide is how we want to manage our keys:

- We can copy our keys from Windows to Linux. This is the least amount of configuration, but we need to keep track of our private keys in more than one place.

- We can share the same file on both Windows and Linux. This requires a bit more configuration, but it means all of our private keys are in one place.

We'll cover both options.

Copying keys from Windows to Linux

To copy our keys from Windows 10 to WSL2 Linux, open up a new Linux tab (**Ubuntu**, for example) and copy the keys to our ~/.ssh directory, creating it if it doesn't already exist:

```
mkdir ~/.ssh
cd ~/.ssh
cp /mnt/c/Users/username/.ssh/id_* .
```

Once copying is complete, the files may have the wrong **Linux permissions**. This is because they were copied over from Windows 10, which does not have the concept of Linux permissions. SSH requires our private keys to have very restrictive permissions, to prevent other users from seeing our keys. We can correct the permissions with the following commands:

```
sudo chown username:username id_*
sudo chmod 600 id_*
```

In the preceding command, replace the word username with the local user's username. We can see an example output in the following screenshot:

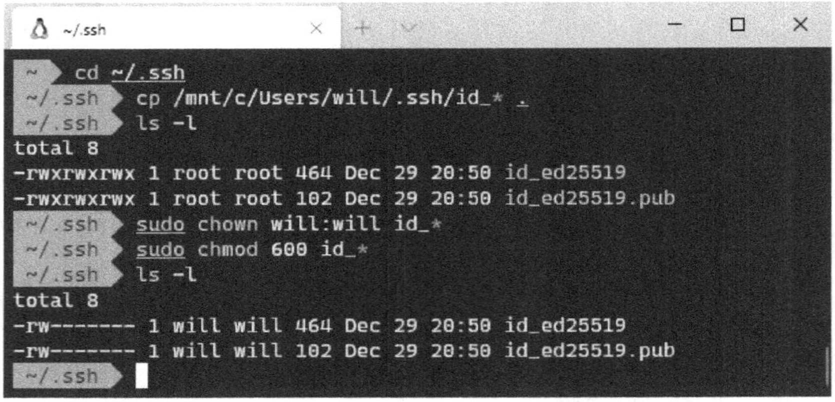

Figure 10.5 – Fixing the permissions after copying our SSH keys

Next, we'll cover the second option: sharing the key file on both Windows 10 and Linux.

Sharing keys in Windows and Linux

If we want to share our keys on both Windows and Linux, we can use a symbolic link for our `.ssh` directory. A symbolic link is similar to a shortcut, in that it's a reference to another place on the filesystem.

First, remove any existing `.ssh` directory (*if one exists, back it up first!*), and then create a symbolic link that points to the `.ssh` directory on Windows:

```
mv ~/.ssh ~/ssh-backup
ln -s /mnt/c/Users/username/.ssh
```

The result can be seen in the following screenshot:

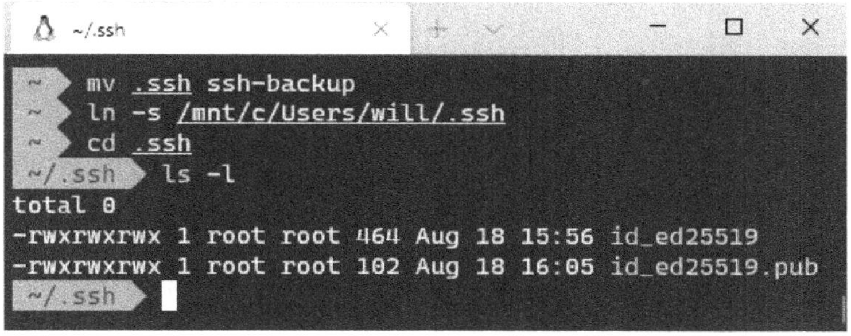

Figure 10.6 – Creating a symbolic link to reuse our keys on Windows and Linux

Now, here's the core of the trick: Using `/etc/wsl.conf` to overlay Linux permissions on Windows filesystems.

As in the previous section, the file permissions of our keys are incorrect; they're too open, and SSH will refuse to work with these insecure files that are readable by everybody.

Unlike the previous section, however, our `chown` and `chmod` commands won't work! This is because we're using an **NTFS** filesystem, the default for Windows. Luckily, WSL2 allows us to layer Linux permissions over the NTFS filesystem by creating a `/etc/wsl.conf` file. Create or edit the file with an editor from inside WSL2. We can use the **nano** editor to edit the file:

```
sudo nano /etc/wsl.conf
```

Add the following contents to the file:

```
[automount]
options = "metadata"
```

To apply the changes, shut down our WSL2 instance by running the `wsl.exe --shutdown` command, and then open a new Windows Terminal tab to start it up again. Now, we're able to use `chown` and `chmod` as normal to fix our file permissions:

```
sudo chown username:username ~/.ssh/id_*
sudo chmod 600 ~/.ssh/id_*
```

Done! We now have the same `.ssh` directory on both Windows and Linux.

Configuring our SSH agent on Linux

Next, let's make it so that when we log in to any server, SSH will add the keys to our SSH agent automatically, and we won't need to repeatedly enter our passphrase.

We'll be using an application named **keychain** to ensure that our SSH agent stays alive across sessions; it's analogous to the Windows Service we used when configuring SSH on Windows. This is especially important for WSL2 in Windows Terminal because each tab is a separate session. We can install keychain from the package repositories with the following command:

```
sudo apt install keychain
```

We can then set it to start automatically by adding the following keychain command to the bottom of our `~/.zshrc` file:

```
eval `keychain --noask --quiet --eval --agents ssh ~/.ssh/id_
ed25519`
```

This will ensure that our SSH agent is always running. Finally, we need to add our SSH keys to the agent. Rather than manually adding the keys, we can configure SSH to automatically add our keys as we use them, by creating a `~/.ssh/config` file with the following contents:

```
Host *
    AddKeysToAgent yes
```

This can be read as *For all hosts (*) add our keys to the SSH agent*. Save this file, and let's give it a try!

We'll try authenticating to GitHub via SSH by running `ssh git@github.com`. As shown in the following screenshot, on the first occasion, we are prompted for our passphrase, but subsequently we are not:

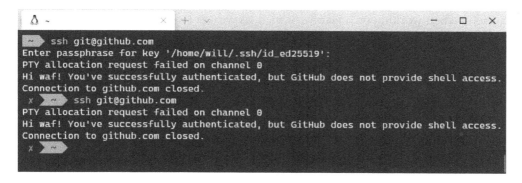

Figure 10.7 – Testing our GitHub authentication. We only need to enter our passphrase the first time

Now, when we open new tabs in Windows Terminal, keychain will ensure that our SSH agent is synchronized across sessions. We've successfully set up a secure, yet convenient, public/private key authentication for SSH and Git!

We've successfully set up Git to have seamless and secure authentication on both Windows 10 and Linux, in Windows Terminal. Next, let's look at some tips on how to use Git effectively in our day-to-day work.

Tips for using Git effectively

The Git command is powerful, and provides many niceties for quick navigation. In this section, we'll cover some tips for speeding up our Git command-line usage.

Switching Git branches with git checkout -

Similar to our tip from the previous chapter, the *hyphen* character can be used as a quick shortcut for toggling between our two most recent Git branches:

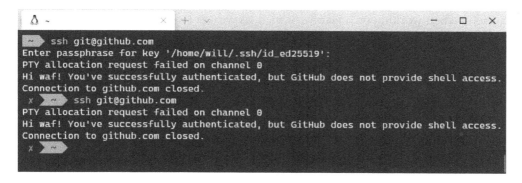

Figure 10.8 – Using "git checkout -" to quickly switch between branches

This is useful when working on a feature branch, as we can switch back and forth between branches without having to type any branch names!

Fixing typos with Git's autocorrect

Ever typed `git chekcout` instead of `git checkout`, or `git stauts` instead of `git status`? Git has an **autocorrect mode**, where, following a configurable timeout, it will automatically run the closest command to what we typed. If there's more than one possible interpretation, it will not run anything:

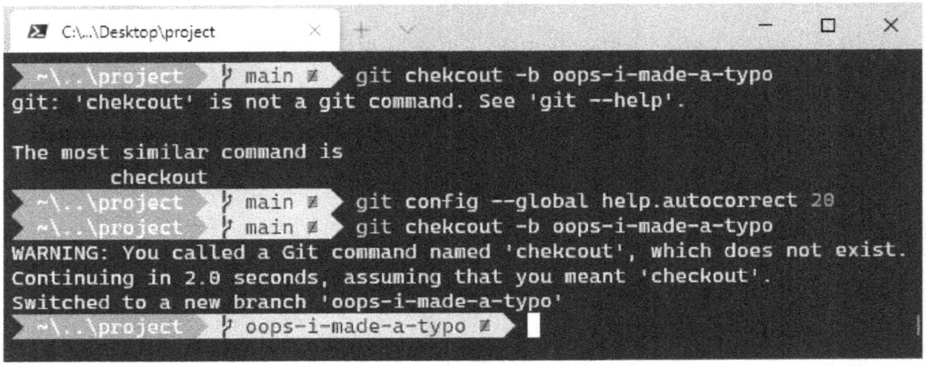

Figure 10.9 – Enabling autocorrect to fix our typos

We can enable this with the following command:

```
git config --global help.autocorrect 20
```

The integer at the end of the command is the timeout, in tenths of seconds. For example, 20 represents *2 seconds*. A value of 0 disables the feature.

Pushing to HEAD

When pushing a Git branch to a remote repository for the first time, we need to specify the desired branch name in the remote repository. If we have a longer branch name, this can be a real pain! We might end up using the mouse to copy and paste the branch name, or trying to use tab completion. Tab completion can also be painful if we have multiple branches with similar prefixes; it still requires a fair amount of typing.

Thankfully, we can use the word HEAD to reference the current branch name. So, rather than having to type the following:

```
git push origin some-long-branch-name
```

We can simply type this:

```
git push origin HEAD
```

The word HEAD is known as a **symbolic ref**. We can see what HEAD currently refers to by running git symbolic-ref HEAD:

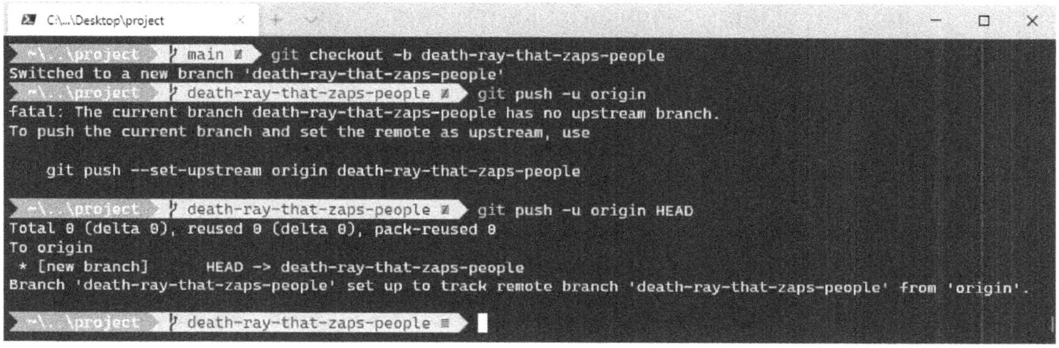

Figure 10.10 – Using HEAD to avoid typing our branch name

Git aliases and command aliases

Git supports two different types of **aliases** for reducing the number of characters we need to type. These aliases can be used to both shorten existing commands and create totally new commands.

The first type of alias is called a **Git Alias** and can be used to shorten existing Git commands. For example, let's say we are often getting the current status of a Git repository, with the git status command. We can shorten this command to git s by setting the following alias:

```
git config --global alias.s status
```

Aliases can include command-line flags, so we can use it to shorten lengthy Git commands. For example, the following command creates the alias git graph, which represents a longer, less memorable log command:

```
git config --global alias.graph 'log --all --decorate --oneline --graph'
```

The second type of alias is called a **Command Alias**, and is prefixed with an exclamation point. Whereas **Git Aliases** only shortened single Git subcommands, **Command Aliases** work on shell commands and can include multiple Git commands.

For example, let's chain together multiple Git commands to create a new `git checkpoint` command, which we can run periodically to ensure that we always have a backup of our changes. This command will save all of our current changes into a temporary commit. We can make multiple checkpoints as we make changes, which will result in multiple temporary commits. Later, when we're ready to share our changes with other developers, we can squash these multiple commits into more logical, understandable commits with the `git rebase` command. This way, we ensure that we always have a backup of our work.

We can create the `git checkpoint` command by setting the following command alias. The first character of the alias is an exclamation point, which tells Git that the rest of the alias is a shell command:

```
git config --global alias.checkpoint '!git add -A && git commit
-m "_checkpoint_"'
```

We've been setting global aliases with the `--global` flag, so all the aliases are stored in our `~/.gitconfig` file. We could also set per-repository aliases by omitting the `--global` flag, in which case they'd be stored in our repository directory, under `.git/config`.

Tig

Certain Git operations are easier with a more graphical representation—after all, Git itself is a graph of commits! Many Git GUI tools are available, and can add real value to our workflow.

The **Tig** program is one such tool, and it runs inside Windows Terminal. Tig was installed automatically when we installed Git for Windows. This tool can browse commits, render Git blames, navigate our stashes, and more.

For example, if we wanted to view a log of commits, and easily see the contents of each commit, we can run the `tig` command in our Git repository. Tig will open a master/details view of our commits, so we can easily see the details of each commit:

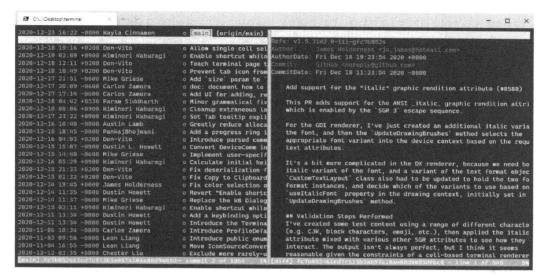

Figure 10.11 – The "tig" tool, showing a log of commits

If the `tig` command was not found, make sure that Git was installed with the **Use git and optional Unix tools from the Command Prompt** option, as covered earlier in this chapter.

Tig has many useful subcommands, which are documented online at `https://jonas.github.io/tig/doc/tig.1.html`. Three of the more interesting subcommands are as follows:

1. `tig stash`: If there are any stashes in the repository, Tig can browse these stashes and show the contents of each stash.

2. `tig status`: This command allows us to view the current status of the repository and interactively run `git add` / `git restore` on files, so we can select which files will be included in our next commit.

3. `tig blame <filename>`: Running this command will launch a built-in file blame viewer, where we can understand how a file changed over time.

Viewing files on different branches

Sometimes, we'll be working on a branch, and want to refer to a file in another branch. We could make a new commit or stash, and then switch branches, but that's a heavyweight, slower way to operate. Git has several ways of viewing files on different branches, without needing to interrupt our work on the current branch.

The easiest way is to run `git gui browser branch-name` from the repository root, which will open a file browser with the contents of the branch `branch-name`. We can navigate to our file, and open it in blame view, all without needing to switch branches.

Alternately, we could run `git show branch-name:path/to/file.txt`. This would display the file inside the terminal, without requiring a graphical user interface.

git reflog

Our final tip for using Git is **git reflog**. The `git reflog` command shows us a view of all changes to any reference in our local repository. This ends up being an incredibly useful way to understand the current state of the repository, and to retrieve *lost commits* that are no longer referenced in any branch:

```
cc8be84 (HEAD -> named-pipe-integration) HEAD@{0}: commit: add visual studio integration
eefa00c HEAD@{1}: checkout: moving from master to named-pipe-integration
e433ad0 (origin/master, origin/HEAD, master) HEAD@{2}: commit (amend): add beginning of unit tests for ViewModelService
d372ae7 HEAD@{3}: commit: add beginning of unit tests for ViewModelService
7db3102 HEAD@{4}: checkout: moving from named-pipe-integration to master
eefa00c HEAD@{5}: commit (amend): add named pipe functionality for sending lines to the REPL
dfd81dd HEAD@{6}: commit: add named pipe functionality for sending lines to the REPL
7db3102 HEAD@{7}: checkout: moving from master to named-pipe-integration
7db3102 HEAD@{8}: commit (amend): replace FileIO delegates with class
e1a33e8 HEAD@{9}: commit: replace FileIO delegates with class
eb51fe3 HEAD@{10}: commit (amend): slightly better way of detecting .NET Core install path
bbed876 HEAD@{11}: commit: slightly better way of detecting .NET Core install path
7c0b566 HEAD@{12}: reset: moving to origin
3e324ac (tag: v0.1.9) HEAD@{13}: reset: moving to HEAD
```

Figure 10.12 – Output from the git reflog command

By way of a light-hearted example, let's say we just came back from vacation and can't remember any of our branch names! We can run `git reflog` on our local repository, and it will show us all of the branches that were recently checked out, and how we were moving between them before our vacation started.

By way of a less light-hearted example, let's say we had a `git rebase` go awry, and accidentally lost some crucial commits. They're no longer in any of our branches! In this case, we can run `git reflog`, find the commit right before our rebase, and then reset our repository directly to that commit's hash.

Now that we've covered how to use Git effectively, let's look at some GitHub-specific tips.

Using GitHub from Windows Terminal

GitHub is an excellent website for software collaboration. GitHub provides hosting for Git repositories, as well as web-based project management tools such as bug trackers and software release management.

One downside is that many of its features, such as **Pull Requests**, are web-based. This generally requires us to point and click on the website, and switch back and forth between a browser and a terminal. This back-and-forth switching can get annoying and inefficient.

GitHub has an official command-line client called gh. As of 2020, this tool is showing promise, but it's far from a full-fledged replacement for using the website. That being said, it's still useful in certain scenarios, which we'll cover in this section.

Specifically, we'll cover the following command-line workflows:

- Creating repositories
- Viewing pull requests
- Checking out pull request branches

gh supports many additional features, such as creating pull requests, but they don't quite provide the productivity boosts we're looking for. However, the tool is rapidly improving, so these features may be worth it in the future.

We can install gh using any of the following means:

1. Download and run the installer from `https://cli.github.com/`.
2. Install it from **chocolatey** via `choco install gh`.
3. Install it with **winget** via `winget install gh`.

Following installation, run `gh auth login` to link the command-line tool to a GitHub account, as shown in the following screenshot:

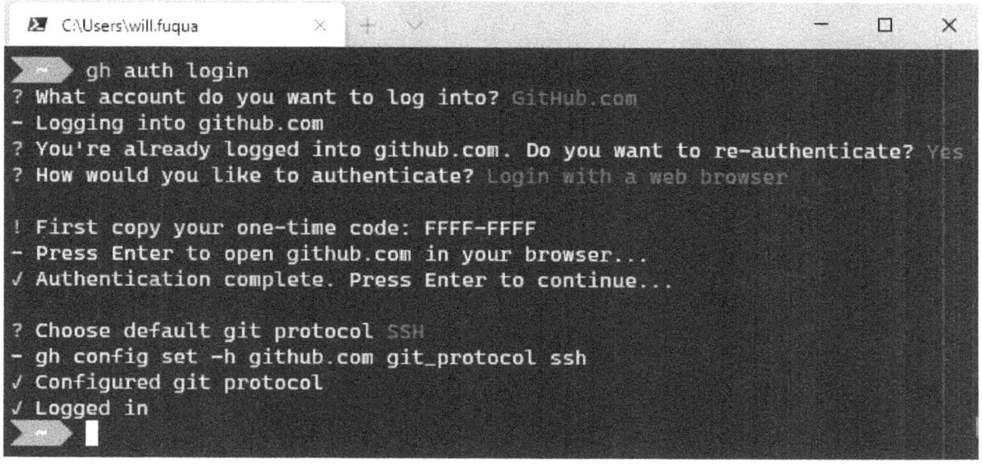

Figure 10.13 – Associating the "gh" tool with our GitHub account

Now, let's run through a couple of ways in which our new gh command can save us some time.

Creating repositories

We'll start out by creating a repository. Normally, this requires two halves of work: using the command line to create the local Git repository, and the browser to create the counterpart on GitHub. We can unify this into a single command with gh.

If we're making a brand new repository, we can issue the following command:

```
gh repo create my-project
```

This will create a new repository on GitHub, named my-project, and also create a local Git repository set up with the remote *origin*. If we already had an existing local Git repository, we could run the following command from inside the repository to create the corresponding GitHub repository:

```
gh repo create
```

The following screenshot shows an example; we start out with a new Git repository, we add a commit, and then create the matching repository on GitHub:

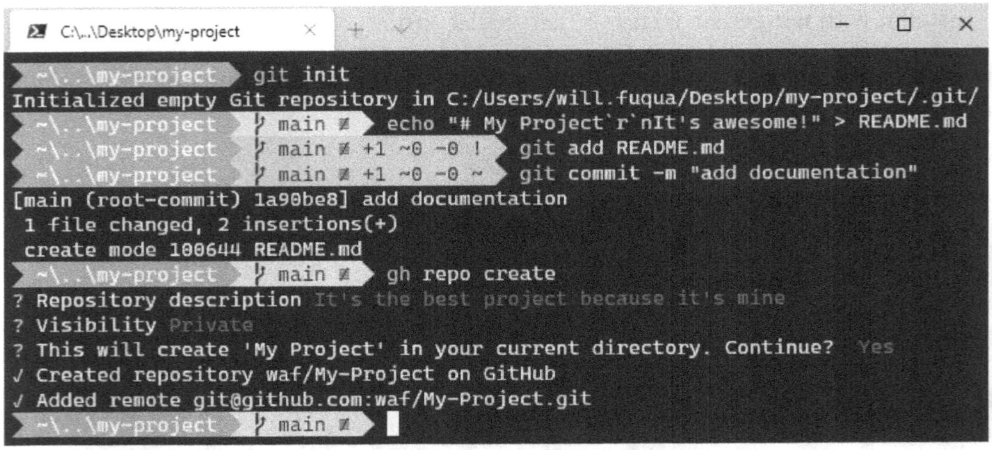

Figure 10.14 – Using Git to create a repository, and gh to create the corresponding GitHub repository

This workflow allows us to stay entirely inside the Window Terminal. If we wanted to browse the repository on GitHub in our web browser, we could run the command gh repo view --web, and our browser will open directly to the repository web page.

Viewing pull requests

Next, we'll look at how we can reduce our terminal and browser switching when dealing with GitHub pull requests. To get started, we'll clone a repository and view its pull requests. For our example, we'll clone the `cli/cli` repository, which is the home of the `gh` tool. We can get the exact command-line invocation from the repository page, as shown in the following screenshot:

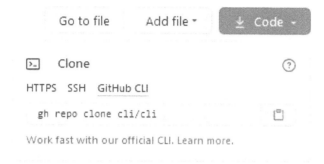

Figure 10.15 – GitHub shows the gh command to clone a repository

After it's cloned, we can list the open pull requests in the repository with the following command:

```
gh pr list
```

For our `cli/cli` repository, we can see a list of the open pull requests in the following screenshot:

```
~\..\cli    trunk ≡   gh pr list

Showing 30 of 41 open pull requests in cli/cli

#2698   view: Add missing newline                camelid:view-newline
#2686   Allow dependabot to keep github action...  jlosito:dependabot-config
#2683   fix: escape browser env variable          sh7dm:escape-browser-env
#2671   [repo/create] Create local repo dir wi...  xhqr:create_local_repo
#2664   Print friendly error when 'gh gist <co...  cristiand391:gist-friendly-error
#2660   Correct remote sort order                 rxfork:correct-remote-sort-order
#2658   Clarify pre-existing token env var err...  drewrisinger:dr-pr-issue-2304-ghtoken-...
#2656   Add final newline back to `pr view`       mxmeinhold:pr-view-newline
#2652   hackday: project support brainstorm       hack20-11
#2650   Extract the oauth package into a separ...  auth-extract
#2630   Respect system/user timezone in API re...  cristiand391:api-respect-timezone
```

Figure 10.16 – The list of pull requests shown by the gh pr list

Like the previous section's `repo view` command, we can also view this pull request list in the browser by adding the `--web` flag (in other words, `gh pr list --web`). Many commands in `gh` support this flag.

Checking out Pull Requests

Finally, we'll cover checking out a branch from a pull request. For example, if we wanted to check out the branch for pull request #2683 from *Figure 10.16*, we could run the following command:

```
gh pr checkout 2683
```

`gh` will then look up the branch name for pull request #2683 and check out that branch for us.

The `gh` command has much more functionality than we've covered here, but the commands we've covered here are the ones that can have the most impact on our command-line workflow. Check out all available functionality at `https://cli.github.com/manual/`.

Summary

In this chapter, we reviewed how to set up Git and ssh-agent to provide a nice command-line experience in Windows Terminal. On Windows, we used the built-in SSH clients, avoiding the need for any third-party utilities. On Linux under WSL2, we used keychain to manage our ssh-agent sessions. We also covered how to share public/private keys across Windows and WSL2.

After that, we covered some tips for using Git quickly and effectively. We finished up by covering Tig, a graphical command-line Git browser bundled in our Git installation, as well as `gh`, a tool for managing our GitHub repositories without leaving Windows Terminal.

In the next chapter, we'll see how to use Windows Terminal effectively when building frontend applications using **React**.

11
Building web applications with React

In this chapter, we'll see how Windows Terminal can be used in modern development workflows. We'll build a small web application using **React**, a popular frontend JavaScript framework from Facebook. Windows Terminal will be one of the main tools in our toolbox.

We'll be using the experience we gained in previous chapters to both develop and run our application on Ubuntu in the **Windows Subsystem for Linux (WSL2)**. We're using Ubuntu because many JavaScript libraries tend to treat Windows 10 as an unfortunate second-class citizen, with Windows-specific issues remaining unfixed. We'll sidestep any compatibility issues with Windows 10 by using WSL2, and have a first-class development experience.

To keep this chapter concise and to the point, we won't be including a full tutorial on React, though we will explain some basic concepts along the way. The principles and techniques we cover in this chapter are generalizable to other technologies, such as **Rust** and **Python**, too.

We'll cover the following topics:

- Installing Node.js in WSL2

- Adding a Node.js profile to Windows Terminal

- Creating a React app

- Developing in WSL2

- Developing with a modern workflow

Technical requirements

In this section, we'll need both **Visual Studio Code** and WSL2 installed. Visual Studio Code should be at least **version 1.35**, and our Linux distribution running inside WSL2 should have all the recent updates applied. The Windows Terminal `settings.json` file and the full client-side application we develop in this chapter are available at `https://github.com/PacktPublishing/Windows-Terminal-Tips-Tricks/tree/main/Chapter 11`.

Installing Node.js in WSL2

Node.js is a popular **JavaScript runtime environment**, and can be used for both backend and frontend development. In this chapter we'll be using it for frontend development; it will manage our library dependencies, compile and check our code, and provide modern developer tools that will help us build applications.

We'll be installing Node.js on Ubuntu, under WSL2. While Node.js development is perfectly possible on Windows and PowerShell, it can lead to dependency headaches with packages like `node_gyp` and SASS. By using WSL2, we'll avoid these issues, and demonstrate how to develop with Windows Terminal and WSL2. The patterns we cover here will extend to developing in other programming languages on WSL2 as well. In *Chapter 12, Building REST APIs with C# and Windows Terminal*, we'll cover a Windows and PowerShell development workflow with Windows Terminal.

While Node.js is available in the standard Ubuntu package repositories, it tends to be out of date. As of 2020, the package repositories contain Node.js version 12, while Node.js is currently at version 15. Instead of installing an older release, we'll install the newest release using the Ubuntu package repository provided by **NodeSource**, a company that is a large part of the Node.js community. More about this package repository can be found at `https://github.com/nodesource/distributions`:

1. Open a new Ubuntu tab in Windows Terminal.

2. Download the installation script by running the following:

   ```
   wget https://deb.nodesource.com/setup_current.x
   ```

   If desired, read through the script. It will add the NodeSource package repository to our system.

3. Run the script as root with the following:

   ```
   sudo bash setup_current.x
   ```

4. After the script completes, install Node.js by running the following:

   ```
   sudo apt install nodejs
   ```

5. Verify that Node.js was installed by running the following:

   ```
   node -v
   ```

   If everything's OK, the preceding command will print out a Node.js version number:

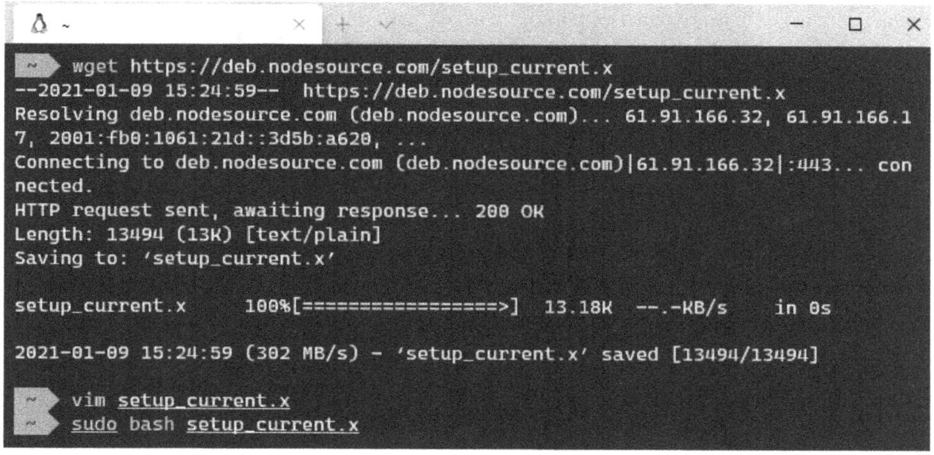

Figure 11.1 – Downloading, reading, and preparing to run the Node.js script

> **Note**
> Using the NodeSource repository is the easiest way to get started with the latest version of Node.js. A downside, however, is that it installs a single version of Node.js on our system. This is usually fine, but can cause problems if we have multiple different applications that all require different versions of Node.js.
> In this scenario, we can use the Node Version Manager available at `https://github.com/nvm-sh/nvm`.

Now that Node.js is installed, let's see how to use it from Windows Terminal.

Adding a Node.js profile to Windows Terminal

Node.js can run our code in two different ways: by reading JavaScript code inside files, or by processing JavaScript code in an **interactive session**. We'll explore the former way later in the chapter as we build our application, and explore the latter way now. The interactive session lets us evaluate JavaScript statements for quick experimentation, similar to a shell. We can add this as a tab or pane in Windows Terminal:

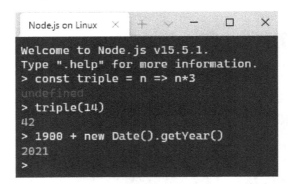

Figure 11.2 – Experimenting with JavaScript in an interactive Node.js session

This can be useful to get instant feedback about JavaScript in the Node.js environment; we can define and iterate on functions, play around with JavaScript syntax, better understand APIs, and more!

The tricky part here is that we installed Node.js in Ubuntu, and we want to access it as a Windows Terminal tab, which is a Windows 10 application. To bridge this gap, we can use the **wsl** utility that we covered in *Chapter 9, Tips for Using Ubuntu like an Expert*.

We can add the following profile definition to our Windows Terminal `settings.json` file (which can be opened by pressing *Ctrl + Shift + ,*). As a reminder, we add this to the `profiles.list` section, and the specific value of the `guid` property does not matter, as long as it's unique:

```
{
    "guid": "{6b1d74e3-843b-4415-88e0-5eead8c49af0}",
    "name": "Node.js on Linux",
    "commandline": "wsl node"
},
```

After saving the file, we'll be able to click to launch **Node.js on Linux** as a tab in Windows Terminal:

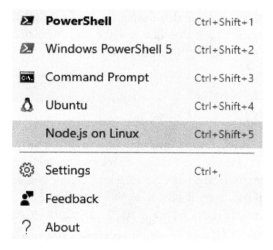

Figure 11.3 – Node.js on Linux as an available Windows Terminal tab

> **Note**
>
> If the `node` command is not found when opening this profile, make sure Ubuntu is set as the default WSL2 distribution by running `wsl --set-default Ubuntu`. The default might be set to another distribution that does not have Node.js installed.

Now that we've set up our Node.js environment, let's create an app! This new **Node.js on Linux** tab will be useful as we're building our application.

Creating a React app

In this section, we'll create a web application using React. We'll use React because it's the most popular frontend framework, and is used by many real-world applications. By using React, we'll ensure that our frontend development workflow with Windows Terminal can handle real-world scenarios.

To get started, we'll use the **create-react-app** generator to create our initial application. This generator will install the required Node.js packages into our project and create a basic starting point for us. From Windows Terminal, open a new Ubuntu tab, navigate to the home directory, and run the following command:

```
npx create-react-app my-app
```

The **npx** tool, provided by our Node.js installation, will install the `create-react-app` package, and then immediately execute this tool at the command line. It will download a large number of dependencies, so it may take a while on slower network connections. When it's done, we'll have our basic application ready to run. Run it with the following commands:

```
cd my-app
npm start
```

When the application runs, it will launch our application in the browser. Our browser is running in Windows, but accessing the Node.js development server running in Ubuntu. In our example, it's running on `http://localhost:3000`. We could also use the real IP of our WSL2 virtual machine; it's listed as the network address displayed in the terminal output. In our example that's `http://172.18.222.198:3000`:

Figure 11.4 – Left: Windows Terminal building and serving our web app; right: our app in the browser

We'll pause here and set up our JavaScript development environment. After we're all set up, we'll come back to this starting point and finish building our application on top of it.

Developing in WSL2

So far, our WSL2 experience has been mostly text-based—fitting for a book on Windows Terminal! While this has served us nicely so far, in this section we'll explore using **Visual Studio Code** as our code editor and debugger, alongside Windows Terminal.

This presents an interesting challenge. Microsoft's guidance is to prefer editing files on the Linux filesystem with Linux applications, as this has the fastest filesystem performance. We would be at a disadvantage if we tried to use Visual Studio Code from Windows 10. It might work, but it'd be a slower and more frustrating experience.

We can fix this by using Microsoft's **Remote - WSL** extension for Visual Studio Code. This extension automatically installs a server into our WSL2 environment, which interacts with our Linux filesystem. Visual Studio Code on Windows 10 then uses a local port to communicate with this server. This process is shown in the following diagram:

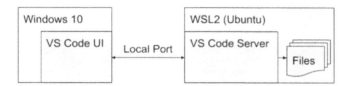

Figure 11.5 – Visual Studio Code's client/server architecture for accessing files in WSL2

It's straightforward to set up—simply navigate to our application directory (my-app, which we created in the previous section) in WSL2 and launch it using the code . command.

In most cases, when Visual Studio launches, it will automatically install the required *Remote - WSL* extension. If it doesn't, we can install it manually from the extensions side panel in Visual Studio Code.

When Visual Studio Code is launched from WSL2, it will open our project and connect to the server running inside WSL2, as seen in the following image. Note the **WSL: Ubuntu** text both in the status bar and in the file explorer:

Figure 11.6 – Visual Studio Code running in WSL2 mode

Once we have Visual Studio Code running in WSL2 mode, we can configure it to talk with our web application. This will allow us to debug our application using Visual Studio Code's debugger tools.

We can configure Visual Studio Code to debug our application by adding a `.vscode/launch.json` file, which controls how Visual Studio Code launches the debugger. Go to **Run | Add Configuration...**, and select **Chrome**:

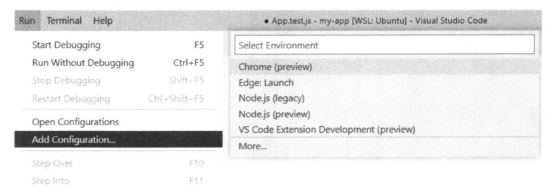

Figure 11.7 – Adding a launch.json file for debugging our web application

This will autogenerate a `launch.json` file for us. Recall that when we started our application with `npm start`, it started on the `http://localhost:3000` URL. Ensure that the `url` property in this file matches:

```
{} launch.json  ●
.vscode > {} launch.json > Launch Targets > {} Launch Chrome against localhost
   1    {
   2          // Use IntelliSense to learn about possible attributes.
   3          // Hover to view descriptions of existing attributes.
   4          // For more information, visit: https://go.microsoft.com/fwlink/?linkid=830387
   5          "version": "0.2.0",
   6          "configurations": [
   7              {
   8                  "type": "pwa-chrome",
   9                  "request": "launch",
  10                  "name": "Launch Chrome against localhost",
  11                  "url": "http://localhost:3000",
  12                  "webRoot": "${workspaceFolder}"
  13              }
  14          ]
  15    }
```

Figure 11.8 – Updating our launch.json's url field to match our web application's URL

Now, let's make sure it's all working together:

1. From Windows Terminal, run `npm start` to start our application.

2. From Visual Studio Code, press the *F5* key to launch the debugger.

3. From Visual Studio Code, navigate to the `src/App.js` file and change the line that says `Edit <code>src/App.js</code> and save to reload` to another message. For example, it could say `Hello from WSL2!`.

4. Save, and verify that the browser automatically refreshes to show the updated message:

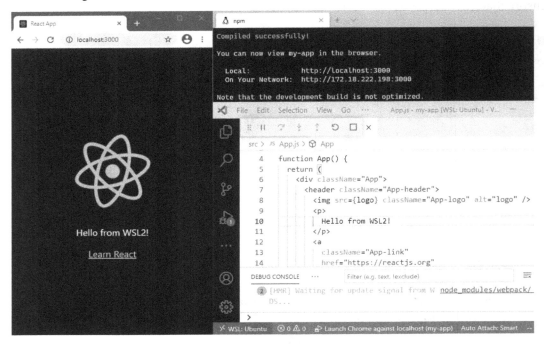

Figure 11.9 – Left: our web application in the browser; right: our Windows Terminal and Visual Studio Code windows

We've now fully set up our Node.js development. Let's use it to build our application!

Developing with a modern workflow

Let's build a very simple live-updating clock application, to exercise our development environment and demonstrate a modern development workflow with Windows Terminal.

For a clock application, the JavaScript `Date` object will be important, so we'll set up our Windows Terminal with a good layout for experimenting with this object and its functions.

Figure 11.10 shows our desired pane layout. It has panes for monitoring our application's build, automated tests, and our interactive Node.js session. We can create it with the following steps:

1. Create a new tab with Ubuntu running in WSL2. Navigate to our `my-app` directory, and run `npm start`.

2. Create a new pane with our Node.js interactive session, by holding down the *Alt* key and clicking on our **Node.js on Linux** profile.

3. Create a new pane with Ubuntu, navigate to our `my-app` directory, and run `npm test`:

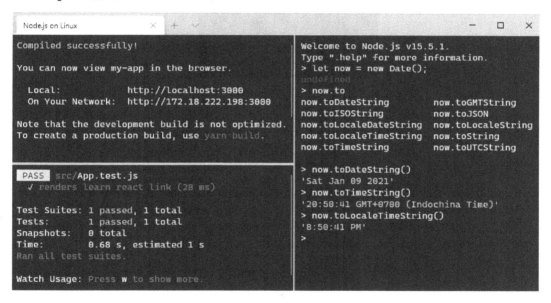

Figure 11.10 – Our Windows Terminal with three Node.js panes – Top left: npm start; bottom left: npm test; right: Node.js interactive session

Next, open Visual Studio Code. If it's not already in WSL2 mode, we can click the ⩽ icon in the bottom left of the status bar, and select **Open Folder in WSL** to open our `my-app` folder. Open the debugger by pressing the *F5* key, and we're ready to code!

We'll create the following clock application, which shows the current time and updates every second:

Figure 11.11 – Our end goal: a clock that updates every second with the current time

This simple application will keep track of a single piece of **state**: the current time. In Visual Studio Code, open the src/App.js and add the following import at the top of the file:

```
import { useState } from "react";
```

When we call this useState function, it will produce two new functions, a *getter function* and a *setter function*, which we will use to get and set the current time in our clock application. Note that as soon as we add the preceding import statement and save the file, we'll get the following warning in our Windows Terminal:

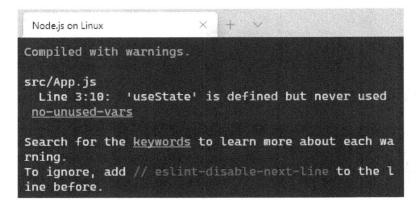

Figure 11.12 – An "unused variable" warning in Windows Terminal

We're being warned that we're importing the `useState` function, but not yet using it. Let's fix that warning by calling this function to create our getter and setter for the current time. We can add it right below the `function App()` line:

```
function App() {
  const [currentTime, setCurrentTime] = useState(new Date());
  return (
```

This creates our getter function, `currentTime`, and our setter function, `setCurrentTime`, with an initial value of the current time (`new Date()`). These two functions will manage our application state.

We can then display the current time by calling our `currentTime` function inside the HTML in our `App` function. At this point, we need to decide how we want to represent the date in our app. Do we want to include the current date? Or just the time? Do we want to include the time zone? JavaScript has convenient functions for displaying the time just the way we want. We can experiment in our **Node.js on Linux** Windows Terminal pane, which we set up earlier in this section:

```
Welcome to Node.js v15.5.1.
Type ".help" for more information.
> let now = new Date();
undefined
> now.to
now.toDateString        now.toGMTString
now.toISOString         now.toJSON
now.toLocaleDateString  now.toLocaleString
now.toLocaleTimeString  now.toString
now.toTimeString        now.toUTCString

> now.toDateString()
'Sat Jan 09 2021'
> now.toTimeString()
'20:50:41 GMT+0700 (Indochina Time)'
> now.toLocaleTimeString()
'8:50:41 PM'
>
```

Figure 11.13 – Experimenting with the Date object to find a good representation for our clock

The `toLocaleTimeString` function looks reasonable, so we can update the `<p>` tag inside the App function to use it as follows:

```
<p>
  The current time is {currentTime.toLocaleTimeString()}
</p>
```

Now, when we look at our clock application, we'll see the current time. However, it won't be updating! If we switch back to our Windows Terminal, we'll see another warning:

```
Compiled with warnings.

src/App.js
  Line 7:23:  'setCurrentTime' is assigned a value but never used  no-unused-vars
```

Figure 11.14 – A warning in Windows Terminal about an unused variable in our application

It's a warning that we never called the `setCurrentTime` function. Because we're not periodically calling it, the time in our application is not updating. We'll want to call this `setCurrentTime` function once a second, which we can do with another React function named `useEffect`. This function is used to tell React that we have a **side effect** that should run, like a timer event or network call, so React will regenerate our HTML as required.

We can import this function by updating our `import` statement at the top of the file:

```
import { useEffect, useState } from "react";
```

And then we call it inside our App function:

```
useEffect(() =>
  setTimeout(() => setCurrentTime(new Date()), 1000)
);
```

This will use JavaScript's `setTimeout` function to call our `setCurrentTime` setter function every second (1,000 milliseconds), providing a new value for the current date and time (`new Date()`).

> **Note**
>
> In a more complex application, we might want to update our `useEffect` function to contain a `clearTimeout` function call as well, so our timer can be stopped if the clock isn't being shown. However, as our application is so simple, we won't worry about that detail for now.

Now, we can check our Windows Terminal to make sure that we don't have any warnings or errors, and then view our application, which is now a functioning clock application:

Figure 11.15 – Our finished web application

We've now developed a simple frontend application, using Visual Studio Code and Windows Terminal. Visual Studio Code was our main editor, and Windows Terminal supported with the error reporting, testing, and experimentation.

Summary

In this chapter, we showed how Windows Terminal can be used to set up a first-class Node.js development environment in WSL2. We used it to install Node.js, and then run the `create-react-app` command to install dependencies and set up a basic application. We also used it to launch Visual Studio Code in the WSL2 development mode.

After that, we showed how to use Windows Terminal during development, by opening panes that provide quick access to important information. We also set up an interactive Node.js session from within WSL2, so we could experiment with the JavaScript `Date` object and other parts of JavaScript.

Now that we've explored using Windows Terminal in frontend development, let's see how it fares at backend development with **.NET Core**.

12
Building REST APIs with C# and Windows Terminal

In this chapter, we'll build a **REST API** and show how Windows Terminal can be an important tool in our workflow. Similar to the previous chapter, where we set up Windows Terminal for our frontend development, this chapter will show how to use Windows Terminal to accelerate our backend development.

A REST API is a popular type of server-side application. These applications are compatible with a wide range of other technologies, such as mobile apps, client-side web applications, and embedded devices. We will create a simple REST API that returns random weather forecasts.

We'll select **C#** as our programming language, running on the **.NET platform**. As we progress through the chapter, we'll set up .NET platform tools for Windows Terminal that make our lives easier and development more efficient. We'll learn how to experiment with C# in the terminal, as well as how to efficiently create, build, run, and test our REST API.

This chapter will cover the following topics, showing how Windows Terminal can help throughout:

- Installing .NET and C#

- Using dotnet script from Windows Terminal

- Generating our REST API

- Testing our REST API

- Making changes to our REST API

- Running unit tests with Windows Terminal

Technical requirements

In this chapter, we'll need to have an editor for C# installed. A good free option is **Visual Studio Code**, which we've been using in previous chapters. If Visual Studio Code is not already installed, it can be downloaded and installed from `https://code.visualstudio.com/`.

Visual Studio can be used in place of Visual Studio Code, but we'll be using Visual Studio Code in many of our examples.

Our `settings.json` file and complete C# application used throughout this chapter are available at `https://github.com/PacktPublishing/Windows-Terminal-Tips-Tricks/tree/main/Chapter 12`.

Installing .NET and C#

The .NET platform is a free and open source technology from Microsoft. It consists of a **runtime**, which defines how our C# programs run cross-platform, as well as a **standard library**, which our C# programs can use. This standard library is quite large, and includes functionality for manipulating dates, connecting to databases, making HTTP requests, and much more.

The concept of the ".NET platform" can be a bit nebulous, so let's make things more concrete by downloading and using it. We can install the latest version of .NET from `https://dotnet.microsoft.com/download/dotnet/`. Most people will want the *Windows / Installer / x64* option:

Build apps - SDK ⓘ

SDK 5.0.102

Included runtimes
.NET Runtime 5.0.2
ASP.NET Core Runtime 5.0.2
.NET Desktop Runtime 5.0.2

Language support
C# 9.0
F# 5.0
Visual Basic 15.9

OS	Installers	Binaries
Linux	Package manager instructions	Arm32 | Arm64 | x64 | x64 Alpine
macOS	x64	x64
Windows	Arm64 | x64 | x86	Arm64 | x64 | x86
All	dotnet-install scripts	

Figure 12.1 – Downloading .NET. Most people will want the Windows Installer for x64 systems

When we run the installer, it will add a `dotnet` command to our system, which we can use from Windows Terminal. We can use this command to create new projects, compile source code, and run the resulting programs. In addition, the `dotnet` command can act as an installer; it can manage our software dependencies and install command-line tools.

To make sure everything's set up correctly, open Windows Terminal and run the `dotnet --version` command. This should print a version number that's *5.0* or greater:

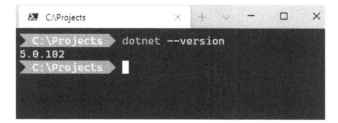

Figure 12.2 – Running dotnet --version to ensure that it installed correctly

Now that we have .NET installed, as well as the `dotnet` command, let's set up our Windows Terminal for .NET development.

Using dotnet script from Windows Terminal

The first thing we'll do is install the `dotnet script` tool, which is a plugin for the `dotnet` command. This tool can run C# code in the terminal, and is useful for experimenting with C# syntax and libraries. We can download and install it using our `dotnet` command:

```
dotnet tool install -g dotnet-script
```

Once the download and installation is complete, we can run it by executing the `dotnet script` command. We can then type C# code and see the result in the terminal:

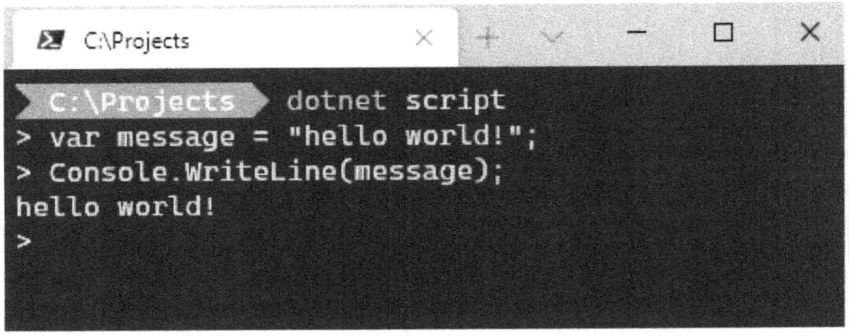

Figure 12.3 – Running C# code in Windows Terminal with dotnet script

We'll be using `dotnet script` later in the chapter, when we're building our REST API. To make it easier to access, we can add it to the Windows Terminal menu by modifying our `settings.json` (*Ctrl + Shift + ,*). In this file, add the following object to the `profiles` section, under the `list` field. The exact value of the `guid` field doesn't matter, as long as it's unique. The `guid` field can even be omitted if the `name` field is unique throughout the file:

```
{
  "guid": "{eae0e5d6-8091-4a5e-af17-12b57cff0337}",
  "name": "C#",
  "commandline": "dotnet script",
  "closeOnExit": "always"
}
```

This will add a *C#* menu option to our Windows Terminal, which we can open from *New Tab Dropdown Menu*:

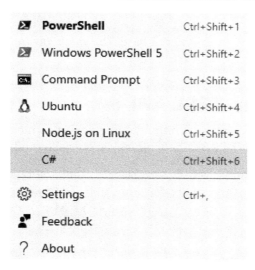

Figure 12.4 – Adding dotnet script to Windows Terminal

Beyond experimenting with C# syntax, this tool can also be used to explore third-party libraries, called **NuGet packages**. For example, say we were curious about the Newtonsoft.Json NuGet package, which is a popular way to parse and serialize JSON. We can download and install version *12.0.3* of Newtonsoft.Json by running the following command:

```
#r "nuget:Newtonsoft.Json, 12.0.3"
```

We can see an example in the following screenshot. Once the package has been downloaded and installed, we can import it by running using Newtonsoft.Json and then experiment with the various JsonConvert APIs it provides. In our example, we're using this library to serialize an object to JSON:

```
> #r "nuget:Newtonsoft.Json, 12.0.3"
> using Newtonsoft.Json;
> JsonConvert.SerializeObject(new { Name = "Bob" })
"{\"Name\":\"Bob\"}"
>
```

Figure 12.5 – Downloading and using NuGet packages in our dotnet script session

By using Windows Terminal in this way, we don't need to create a bunch of small projects just for our experimentation. When we close the terminal tab, there's nothing to clean up, and no small, temporary projects littering our filesystem.

Next, let's start building our application! We'll begin by generating a C# REST API from a template, so we have a solid project as our base. This helps ensure that our Windows Terminal setup works for real-world applications.

Generating our REST API

In this section, we'll use our `dotnet` command to quickly download the required libraries and generate an initial REST API, which we can then modify to suit our needs.

The `dotnet` command includes various templates for different types of projects. To see a list of all templates, we can run the `dotnet new --list` command. One of the templates is named `webapi`, which will generate a REST API for us. We can use this template by running the following command in PowerShell:

```
dotnet new webapi -o App\App.WebApi
```

This will create a new folder, named `App`, that contains our REST API nested inside the `App.WebApi` folder (we'll take advantage of this nested folder structure in future sections). After navigating to the `App\App.WebApi` folder, we can launch our API by running the following command:

```
dotnet watch run
```

Our REST API will start running and open a page in the browser so we can test it, as seen in the following screenshot:

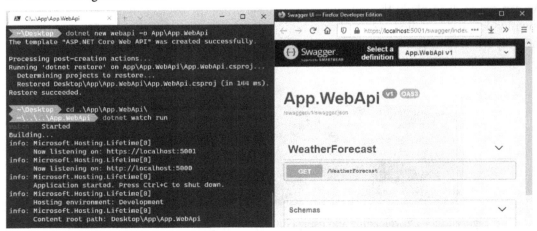

Figure 12.6 – Generating and running our initial REST API

> **Note**
> If the browser displays a security warning when browsing our new website, we can fix it by trusting the development **SSL certificate**. This only needs to be done one time, by issuing the `dotnet dev-certs https --trust` command.

We can call our REST API from the browser by clicking our **/WeatherForecast** link in the browser, then clicking **Try it out**, and finally clicking **Execute**. We'll see it return the following random weather forecasts:

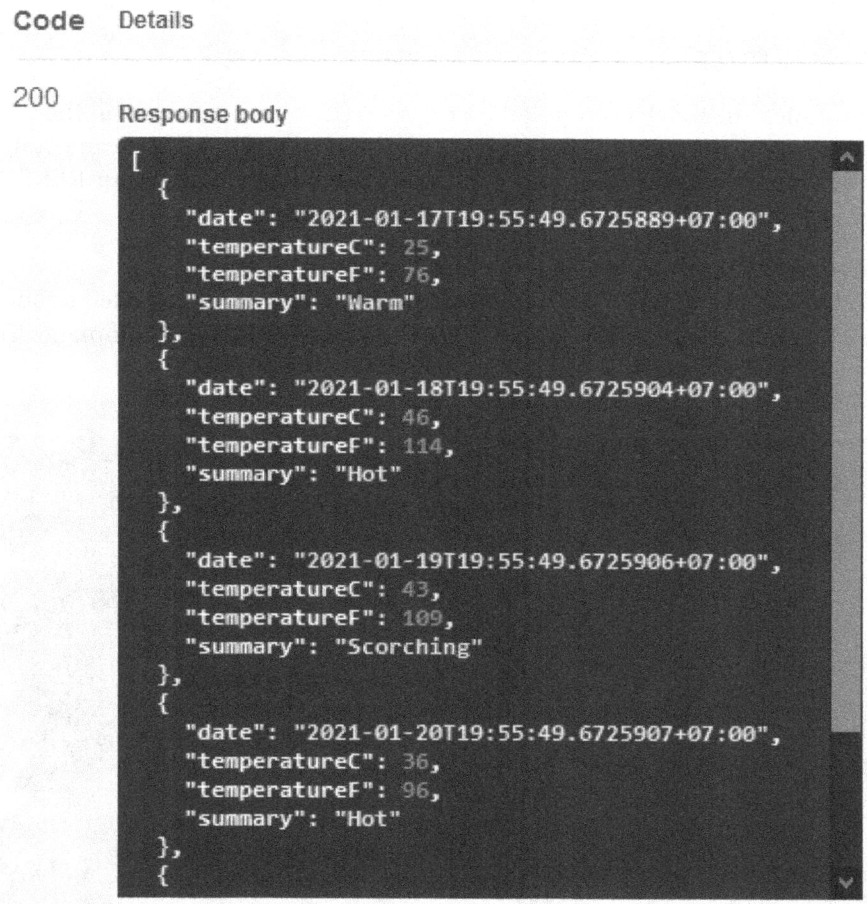

Figure 12.7 – The results of calling HTTP GET on our /WeatherForecast API

Our weather forecasts contain the date of the forecast, the temperature in both Celsius and Fahrenheit, as well as a text summary of the weather condition.

While we can test it in the browser like this, it ends up requiring a bit of repetitive clicking. To fix this, we can also test it from Windows Terminal, which we'll explore in the next section.

Testing our REST API

To test our REST API from Windows Terminal, we can install another dotnet tool: Microsoft's *HTTP REPL*. This tool allows any HTTP API to be tested, regardless of the server-side technology. To install it, run the following command in a new Windows Terminal PowerShell pane:

```
dotnet tool install -g Microsoft.dotnet-httprepl
```

We can then launch the tool by running the `httprepl` command, as seen in the following screenshot. The tool will launch in a *Disconnected* mode, and we can connect to our API by typing the command `connect <url>`, where the URL is our REST API's address (for example, `https://localhost:5001`).

Once we've connected, we can use `ls` to view available resources (like our `WeatherForecast`) and type `cd` to navigate to them. Once we've navigated to our `WeatherForecast` resource, we can type `GET` to run an **HTTP GET** command. This will call our API and return the result:

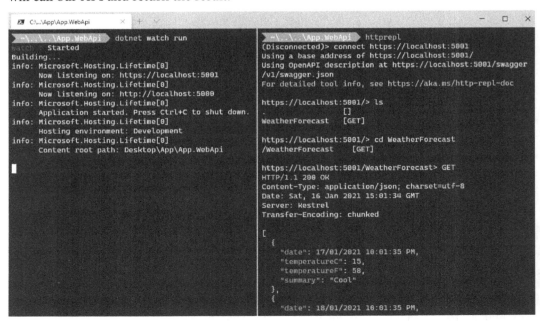

Figure 12.8 – Calling our /WeatherForecast API from Microsoft's HTTP REPL tool

We could add our `httprepl` command to our Windows Terminal with the following entry in our `settings.json` file:

```
{
    "guid": "{93e15e18-8b0e-4a36-b268-0f7408c07c5b}",
    "name": "HTTP REPL",
    "commandline": "httprepl"
}
```

Next, we'll make some changes to our REST API, and see how Windows Terminal helps us test these changes.

Making changes to our REST API

In a previous section, we launched our REST API with the `dotnet watch run` command. The `watch` portion of this command instructs the `dotnet` command to watch our project for changes, and autoreload the application with those changes applied. Let's see this in action!

First, we'll open our `App` folder in Visual Studio Code. Once it's open, navigate to the `App.WebApi\Controllers\WeatherForecastController.cs` file and find where it's generating the weather forecasts:

```
[HttpGet]
public IEnumerable<WeatherForecast> Get()
{
    var rng = new Random();
    return Enumerable
        .Range(1, 5)
        .Select(index => new WeatherForecast
        {
            Date = DateTime.Now.AddDays(index),
            TemperatureC = rng.Next(-20, 55),
            Summary = Summaries[rng.Next(Summaries.Length)]
        })
        .ToArray();
}
```

It's generating five random temperatures between -20 and 55 degrees Celsius, and then randomly selecting a summary. We can make the temperature a little more comfortable by changing the temperature range to start at 15 and end at 30:

```
TemperatureC = rng.Next(15, 30),
```

Save the file, and we'll see our dotnet watch run command automatically reload our application. We can use our httprepl command to issue a few more HTTP GET requests to make sure everything's working OK.

Wait a moment—did we use that rng.Next method correctly? Will it include the numbers 15 and 30 in the possible random numbers, or will it exclude them? Let's open a new pane in Windows Terminal, running our new C# profile, by holding the *Alt* key and clicking on the C# menu option in **New Tab Dropdown Menu**:

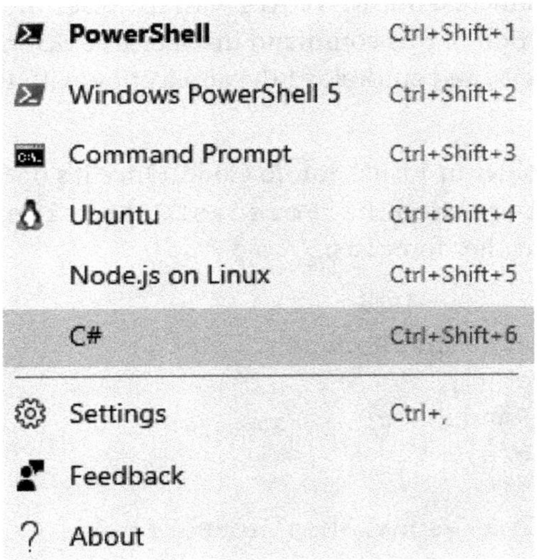

⚡	**PowerShell**	Ctrl+Shift+1
⚡	Windows PowerShell 5	Ctrl+Shift+2
🖥	Command Prompt	Ctrl+Shift+3
🐧	Ubuntu	Ctrl+Shift+4
	Node.js on Linux	Ctrl+Shift+5
	C#	Ctrl+Shift+6
⚙	Settings	Ctrl+,
🗨	Feedback	
?	About	

Figure 12.9 – Opening a C# pane by holding Alt when clicking the C# menu option

We can play with the rng.Next method here, and confirm our suspicions: the lower bound is included, but the upper bound is excluded:

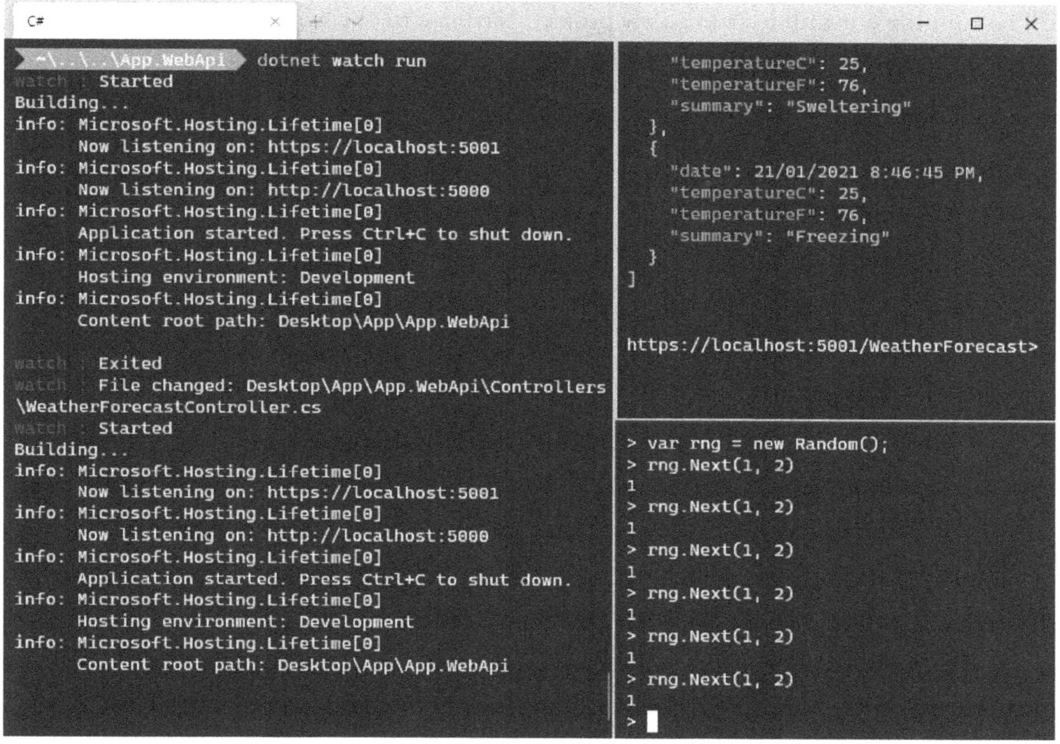

Figure 12.10 – In the lower-right corner, confirming how the rng.Next method works

This means that the line we just changed introduced a bug! We can fix our bug by updating our upper bound to 31, so now we'll generate random numbers from 15 to 30, including both 15 and 30:

```
TemperatureC = rng.Next(15, 31),
```

Save the changes, our API will autoreload, and now we have a working weather forecast API. Windows Terminal is helping us to build and reload our application, test it with the HTTP REPL, and experiment with .NET APIs using our C# Windows Terminal pane.

Running unit tests with Windows Terminal

We almost introduced a bug in the last section, but caught it at the last minute. We were lucky; we might not catch the next bug. Let's set up some **unit tests** that will run automatically and help catch future bugs.

We'll be running our unit tests in a new project. Navigate to our App directory and create a new test project using the following command:

```
dotnet new xunit -o App.Tests
```

This will create a new project for our tests, next to our App.WebApi project. The folder structure should now look like this:

Figure 12.11 – Our generated project structure

We'll want to tell the App.Tests project how to find our App.WebApi project, so it can test the functionality inside. Navigate to the top-level App folder, and run the following command:

```
dotnet add App.Tests reference App.WebApi
```

Next, in Visual Studio Code, open the App.Tests/UnitTest1.cs file, where we'll be writing our automated tests. First, we'll need to import our code that we want to test. Add the following code to the top of the file:

```
using App.WebApi;
```

A good candidate to test is our Celsius to Fahrenheit conversion. Let's add a test that will check that the following conversions always work:

- 25 degrees Celsius should be 77 degrees Fahrenheit.
- 0 degrees Celsius should be 32 degrees Fahrenheit.
- -40 degrees Celsius should be -40 degrees Fahrenheit.

We can do this by adding the following method to our unit test class:

```
[Theory]
[InlineData(25, 77)]
[InlineData(0, 32)]
[InlineData(-40, -40)]
public void WeatherForecast_GivenCelsius_
ShouldConvertToFahrenheit(
    int c,
```

```
        int expectedF)
{

    var forecast = new WeatherForecast { TemperatureC = c };
    Assert.Equal(expectedF, forecast.TemperatureF);
}
```

We can run these tests from Windows Terminal. From the `App\App.Tests` directory, run the following command:

```
dotnet watch test
```

This will run our three temperature conversion unit tests, as shown in the following screenshot:

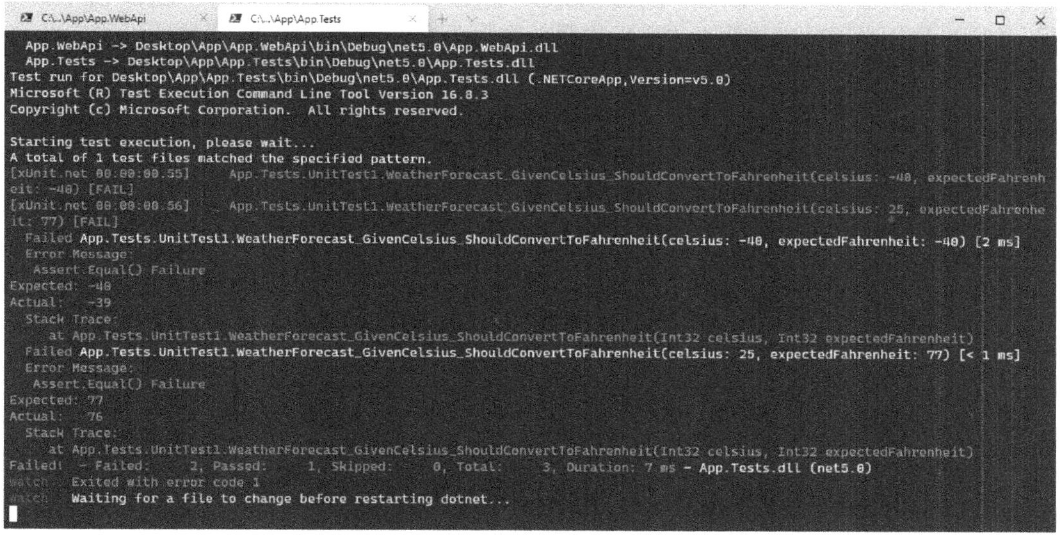

Figure 12.12 – Running our unit tests with the command dotnet watch test. They failed!

Two of the tests failed! As of late 2020, the template from Microsoft has a rounding error in the Celsius to Fahrenheit conversion. It's left as an exercise to you to identify and fix this bug (hint: it's in the `WeatherForecast.cs` file). When the bug is fixed, all three tests will pass and show in a rewarding green color.

Summary

In this chapter, we showed how Windows Terminal can be used in all parts of our workflow when we're developing C# applications.

We used Windows Terminal to generate applications from templates, giving us an initial starting point for our application. We then used Windows Terminal as a core tool for building, running, and testing our application.

We also set up several useful command-line tools. We started out by adding a C# tab to Windows Terminal, using the `dotnet script` tool, which allows us to easily test C# syntax and libraries. We also used the Microsoft HTTP REPL tool to test our Web API.

Now we've built both client-side software (in the previous chapter) and server-side software (in this chapter) with Windows Terminal. Next, we'll look at connecting to remote machines with Windows Terminal, which is a critical step in deploying and managing our software.

13
Connecting to remote systems

So far in this book, we've mostly stayed confined to a single computer. We've developed client-side and server-side applications using Windows Terminal, and the next step is to connect to **remote computers** so we can deploy our applications! In this chapter, we'll break out of our single-machine confines and learn how to connect to both Windows and Linux systems remotely.

We'll start out by comparing the options for connecting remotely and configuring our systems for remote access. We'll then learn how to streamline our remote access with Windows Terminal, **Secure Shell** (**SSH**), and the **Secure Copy Protocol** (**SCP**).

By the end of this chapter, we'll be able to decide between WinRM and SSH remote access, set up both inbound and outbound SSH access on Windows, and take advantage of the shortcuts and conveniences that SSH and SCP provide. We'll cover the following topics:

- Connecting to Windows computers with WinRM and SSH
- Copying files with SCP
- Connecting to Linux machines
- Saving routinely accessed hosts and commands
- Saving remote connections in Windows Terminal

Technical requirements

In *Chapter 10, Using Git and GitHub with Windows Terminal*, we set up SSH authentication for use with Git. This included generating public and private keys, and installing the SSH client on Windows 10. We'll be building on top of that in this chapter.

All the configuration files discussed in this chapter are available online at `https://github.com/PacktPublishing/Windows-Terminal-Tips-Tricks/tree/main/Chapter 13`.

Connecting to Windows computers with WinRM and SSH

In this section, we'll learn how to connect to remote Windows computers with both WinRM and SSH. Historically, the main way to connect to a remote Windows computer was with Remote Desktop. The Remote Desktop application was graphical; it showed the desktop of the remote computer, along with the cursor, icons, and menus. However, many modern Windows servers, such as those running Windows Server Core, are now **headless**—that is, they don't include a graphical user interface at all! This is done to both decrease installation size, and thus the size of updates, as well as to reduce the attack surface of the server. While Remote Desktop can still be used to connect to these headless servers, it only renders a terminal.

Rather than using a graphical application such as Remote Desktop to render a terminal, we can just use Windows Terminal to connect directly to the remote computer, without any graphical programs required. There are two different technologies we can use: **WinRM** and **SSH**. We'll use WinRM to connect to Windows systems, and SSH to connect to both Windows and Linux systems.

Connecting with WinRM

WinRM, which stands for **Windows Remote Management**, is a popular way to connect to Windows computers and is enabled by default on modern Windows Server installations. It's especially suitable for corporate environments as it is managed by Windows Group Policy, the standard way for managing corporate Windows environments.

While the WinRM server is enabled by default on Windows Server, it's disabled on Windows 10. This is normally not an issue as we usually want to connect remotely to servers, not to other clients. Let's take a brief detour and cover how to enable the WinRM server on Windows 10, so we could connect, for example, from our laptop to our desktop computer, both running Windows 10.

To enable the WinRM server on our desktop computer, we can run the following PowerShell command in Windows Terminal, with Administrator privileges:

```
Enable-PSRemoting -SkipNetworkProfileCheck -Force
```

This command will configure the WinRM service to automatically start, and set up a firewall rule to allow inbound connections.

Now that the server is set up, let's try connecting. On the client, open Windows Terminal and run the following command, where <host> is the hostname of the remote machine, and <username> is the username to connect as:

```
Enter-PSSession -ComputerName <host> -Credentials <username>
```

> **Note**
>
> If the value of the ComputerName parameter is localhost, then Windows Terminal must be running with administrator permissions, that is, started via **Run as Administrator**. This is required due to mitigations put in place to fix a security issue (see CVE-2019-0543 in the CVE online database).

If the local network is using Active Directory authentication, this may be enough to connect to the computer. If it's not, then we might see an error similar to the following:

```
ERROR: The WinRM client cannot process the request. If the
authentication scheme is different from Kerberos, or if the
client computer is not joined to a domain, then HTTPS transport
must be used or the destination machine must be added to the
TrustedHosts configuration setting.
```

To fix this, we can add the remote server to our client's TrustedHosts setting. This setting is a comma-delimited list of hostnames, and supports wildcards. We can set the TrustedHosts setting with the following command:

```
Set-Item WSMan:\localhost\Client\TrustedHosts -Value
'my-computer-1,*.my-domain.com'
```

This command would trust the computer with the hostname my-computer-1, and then trust all computers where the hostname ends in .my-domain.com.

Connecting with WinRM is the most suitable option for corporate environments, where we need to rely on defaults and can't necessarily modify the servers we want to connect to. As WinRM is enabled by default, it's often the easiest way to connect. Next, we'll take a look at an alternative and more powerful way of connecting to Windows Servers: SSH.

Connecting to Windows computers with SSH

Recent versions of Windows support connecting over SSH. We set up our SSH client as part of our Git configuration back in *Chapter 10, Using Git and GitHub with Windows Terminal*, and used it to connect to servers running Linux. If the SSH client is not already set up, check out that chapter to get up and running.

In this section, we'll configure the built-in **SSH server** in Windows, so we can use SSH to connect to both Linux and Windows computers. Similar to how we enabled the SSH client, we can enable the SSH server via the **Optional Features** setting in Windows 10. In the Start menu, search for Manage Optional Features, then add the **OpenSSH Server** feature:

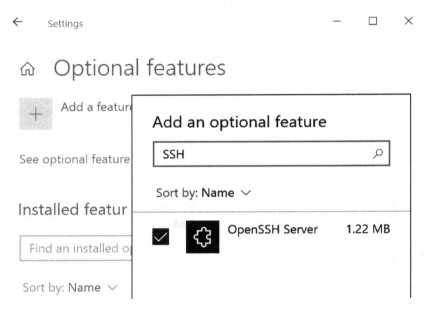

Figure 13.1 – Installing OpenSSH Server in Windows

After it's installed, we can start the **OpenSSH SSH Server** service from the **Services** app, as shown in the following screenshot, and configure it to automatically start on boot (by setting **Startup type** to **Automatic**):

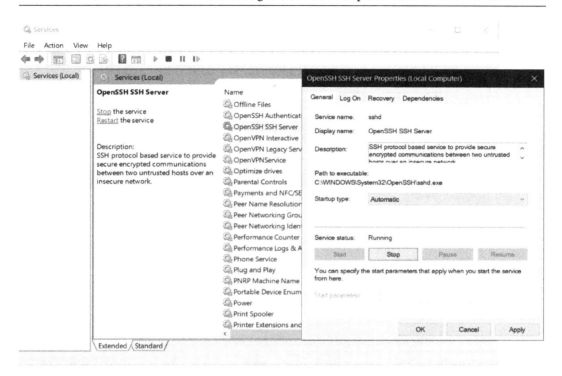

Figure 13.2 – Starting the OpenSSH SSH Server service, and configuring it to launch on startup

After the service is started, we can connect to the server using our SSH client. In Windows Terminal, run the following command to log into the my-username account on the computer named my-server:

```
ssh my-username@my-server
```

We'll be prompted for our password, and upon successful login we'll be at a new Command Prompt instance. Success! Now we can run commands on remote computers.

Changing the default shell

Now that we can successfully connect, let's change the default shell from the Command Prompt to PowerShell Core. We do this with a registry key named `DefaultShell` under `HKEY_LOCAL_MACHINE\SOFTWARE\OpenSSH`, which points to the path of the executable as a string:

```
reg add HKLM\SOFTWARE\OpenSSH /v DefaultShell /d "C:\Program
Files\PowerShell\7\pwsh.exe"
```

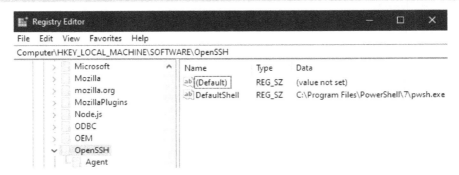

Figure 13.3 – Switching our default SSH shell from the Command Prompt to PowerShell Core

Now, when we log in via SSH, PowerShell Core (`pwsh.exe`) will be launched, instead of the Command Prompt.

Setting up public key authentication

So far we've set up **password authentication**, which is convenient. However, this can leave us open to brute-force attacks on our server, especially if the server is available over the public internet.

We set up our public and private keys in *Chapter 10, Using Git and GitHub with Windows Terminal,* so let's use these keys to authenticate instead. As a reminder, we had two files: our public key file named `id_ed25519.pub` and our private key file named `id_ed25519`. Our private key should never leave our computer, and we can share our public key.

Let's say our username on our local laptop is `Will`, and we want to connect to a server as the user `William`—so we have two slightly different usernames. Our public and private keys would be at the path `C:\Users\Will\.ssh\` on our laptop.

We'll copy the contents of our public key, `id_ed25519.pub`, and paste the contents into the `C:\Users\William\.ssh\authorized_keys` file on the server. Both these files are plain text and can be opened in any text editor, and the `authorized_keys` file can be created if it doesn't exist. This will allow us to log in as `William` on the server:

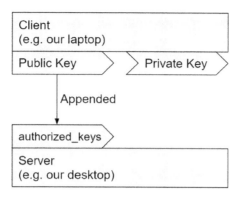

Figure 13.4 – The public key on our client is appended to the authorized_keys file of the remote server

If we're connecting as a user with administrator privileges, we need to put the keys into C:\ProgramData\ssh\administrators_authorized_keys instead (create it if it doesn't exist). This file must be accessible only by the **SYSTEM** user and the **Administrators** group. This means we'll need to disable permission inheritance, via **Properties | Security | Advanced | Change Permissions | Disable Inheritance | Convert Inherited Permissions**, and then remove the **Authenticated Users** group, if it exists. We can see the required permissions for the administrators_authorized_keys file in the following image:

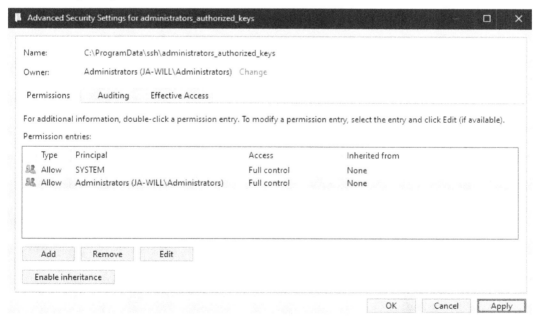

Figure 13.5 – Ensuring our administrators_authorized_keys file has the correct permissions

To make sure everything's working correctly, try connecting via SSH again. If it's all set up correctly we won't be prompted for a password; our public and private key authentication will be used automatically instead.

Once we've verified that the public and private key authentication is working, the final step is to disable password authentication. We can do this by modifying our SSH server's configuration file, located at `C:\ProgramData\ssh\sshd_config`. In this file, we can find the following commented line:

```
#PasswordAuthentication yes
```

Remove the initial comment character (#) to activate the line, and then change `yes` to `no`:

```
PasswordAuthentication no
```

Save the file and restart the **OpenSSH SSH Server** service from the **Services** app. Now, password access will not be allowed, and only users that have key files listed in their `authorized_keys` will be able to connect.

> **Note**
>
> The `sshd_config` file controls many aspects of SSH's behavior, including which users are allowed to connect, and is documented at `https://docs.microsoft.com/en-us/windows-server/administration/openssh/openssh_server_configuration`.

Now that we've successfully set up our Windows server for SSH authentication, let's see how we can interact with it remotely from our client computer.

Copying files with SCP

While SSH allows us to send commands to a remote computer, **SCP** allows us to send files. This can be useful if we want to upload a file to a server as part of an application deploy, or even just to share that file with other people.

The command structure is `scp source destination`, where `source` and `destination` represent either local or remote files. A local file is represented by its file path, and a remote file is represented by `username@server:/path/to/file`.

For example, if we wanted to copy a file from our client computer to a server, we can run the following command:

```
scp my-file.txt william@my-server:/Users/william/Desktop/
```

The preceding command will send our file named `my-file.txt` to the server named `my-server`, after logging in with the username `william`. The destination path will be `/Users/William/Desktop/my-file.txt`.

If we wanted to copy a directory of files instead of a single file, we could use the `-r` command flag to recursively copy an entire directory. For example, if we had a directory containing an application we developed, we could deploy the application to the server with the following command:

```
scp -r MyApp william@server:/inetpub/wwwroot
```

So far, we've been copying files from our computer to some remote server. We can do the opposite, too, and copy files from the remote server to our computer. To do this, we simply swap the order of the two arguments to `scp`. As an example, to copy the `/path/to/source/my-file.txt` file from the remote server to our computer, we would run the following:

```
scp william@server:/path/to/source/my-file.txt my-file.txt
```

Now we can log in with SSH to our remote Windows computer and copy files between our local Windows computer and remote Windows computers. Let's take a brief look at how this works on remote *Linux* computers.

Connecting to Linux machines

To connect to Linux machines, it's exactly the same! We can use our SSH client to remotely connect, SCP to copy files, and `sshd_config` to configure the service's behavior. This is a major benefit of SSH and SCP; a single command works on both Linux and Windows.

The SSH server will need to be installed and running, and this is set up by default on most Linux servers. If it's not already set up, we can install the SSH package from our software repositories. On Ubuntu, that'd be done via the following command:

```
sudo apt install openssh-server
```

Finally, we need to ensure that our public key is in the `~/.ssh/authorized_keys` file, just like we did on Windows.

Now that we can connect to both Windows and Linux, let's see how we can connect more efficiently, and avoid needing to memorize usernames and hostnames.

Saving routinely accessed hosts and commands

So far, we've been typing in our username and server hostname every time we want to connect to a server. As we get more and more servers, or more advanced configuration, we'll want to save these connection details and not have to type them at the command line every time!

Our SSH client will read the `~/.ssh/config` file, which can store a list of hosts and their SSH configuration. This works for both Windows and Linux hosts, and we can provide memorable names for each host. For example, the following configuration will allow us to type `ssh home` and connect to the server with these details:

```
Host "home"
    HostName home-server.example.com
    Port 22
    User William
    IdentityFile ~/.ssh/id_ed25519
```

This can be especially useful if we don't have a hostname, and we need to connect by IP. For example, we can associate the name "router" with the IP `192.168.1.1`, allowing us to type `ssh router` with the following configuration:

```
Host "router"
    HostName 192.168.1.1
    User admin
```

The `Host` field is not limited to single strings. It supports multiple names, for example, if we wanted to allow both `ssh router` and `ssh wifi` to connect to our Wi-Fi router:

```
Host "router", "wifi"
    HostName 192.168.1.1
    User admin
```

It also supports wildcard matching, with `*` matching zero or more characters, and `?` matching a single character. One useful application of this is matching IP addresses; if we had multiple servers, all on the `192.168.10.*` subnet, we could configure the username and private key file for all of the servers with a single configuration:

```
Host "192.168.10.*"
    User web_user
    IdentityFile ~/.ssh/id_test_environment_private_key
```

Finally, we can also invoke commands when we connect, for example, to set the initial working directory for our PowerShell Core shell:

```
Host "desktop"
    HostName 192.168.1.1
    RemoteCommand pwsh -WorkingDirectory /
    RequestTTY yes
```

The `~/.ssh/config` file supports a large number of configuration keys, and is documented online at `https://man.openbsd.org/ssh_config.5`:

```
 1 Host *
 2     AddKeysToAgent yes
 3
 4 Host "home-server"
 5     HostName home-server.example.com
 6     Port 22
 7     User will
 8     IdentityFile ~/.ssh/id_rsa
 9
10 Host ec2-instance
11     HostName 4.15.218.17
12     User ec2-user
13     IdentityFile ~/.ssh/id_ed25519
14
15 # test api servers
16 Host "172.16.16.*"
17     User ubuntu
18     IdentityFile ~/.ssh/id_api
19
20 Host github.com
21     HostName github.com
22     User git
23     IdentityFile ~/.ssh/id_ed25519
```

Figure 13.6 – A sample ~/.ssh/config file

By using our `~/.ssh/config` file, we have a centralized place to store all of our connection details. Next up, we'll reference these connection details in our Windows Terminal, which will give us a nice user interface to quickly launch these sessions.

Starting remote connections in Windows Terminal

Now that we have our `~/.ssh/config` file, it's almost trivial to add our remote connections to Windows Terminal. We don't need to care whether we're connecting to Linux or Windows; the command is the same either way.

Open the settings.json file (*Ctrl + Shift +* ,) and add the remote connections to the profile.list array. Each guid value should be unique, and the command line should point to our hosts that we set up in our ~/.ssh/config file. Alternatively, if the name field is unique throughout the file, we can omit the guid field entirely:

```
// connect to our router, probably running linux
{
    "guid": "{663bb60f-01bb-48f3-b552-176ff3fdc711}",
    "name": "Connect to Router",
    "commandline": "ssh router"
},
// connect to our desktop, running Windows
{
    "guid": "{a24b83df-a269-4439-bc3c-b2f483009624}",
    "name": "Connect to Desktop",
    "commandline": "ssh desktop"
},
```

This configuration results in two items in our menu, and clicking either item will result in a new **Windows Terminal** tab that connects to the remote system:

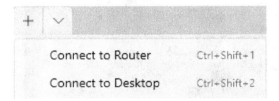

Figure 13.7 – Our remote connections are available in Windows Terminal

Of course, it's possible to not use the ~/.ssh/config file at all, and instead use the command line flags of the ssh command directly in our settings.json file. However, that way we lose the ability to use our SSH configurations in other contexts, such as invoking them from within the terminal, and we also need to deal with some tricky string escapes when embedding our SSH commands into JSON strings.

Summary

In this chapter, we covered connecting to Windows computers with WinRM, and how to enable it if it's not already set up. We also learned how to enable the SSH server on Windows, and how to securely configure it and connect with public/private key authentication.

We also covered client tools such as SSH and SCP, which provide a unified way to work with both Windows and Linux systems. We used our ~/.ssh/config file to keep a record of our servers and their associated configuration, such as IPs, hostnames, and private keys.

Finally, we showed how to integrate all of this with Windows Terminal so we can quickly access remote servers with the press of a button. In the next chapter, we'll move from managing single computers via SSH to managing fleets of servers in the cloud with Windows Terminal.

14
Managing systems in the cloud

In this chapter, we'll continue our theme of working on remote systems and begin connecting to the **cloud**. We'll learn how to connect to **Microsoft Azure**, **Google Cloud**, and **Amazon Web Services** (**AWS**), all within Windows Terminal.

The cloud is an important part of modern development and DevOps workloads; companies are often happy to pay a higher price for increased flexibility and reduced maintenance. With the number of services that clouds provide, it's common to interact with them multiple times per day—so it's worth spending some time optimizing our cloud workflow!

By the end of this chapter, we'll have integrated Microsoft Azure, Google Cloud, and Amazon Web Services into our Windows Terminal. The techniques and patterns we'll learn for these three cloud providers will leave us well equipped to integrate any other cloud providers in the future.

In this chapter, we'll cover the following topics:

- Using Microsoft Azure's Cloud Shell and `az interactive`
- Using Google Cloud Shell and `gcloud interactive`
- Using Amazon Web Services from Windows Terminal

Technical requirements

In this chapter, we'll be using WSL2 to work with both Google Cloud and Amazon Web Services. Instructions for setting up WSL2 are in *Chapter 3, Configuring an Ubuntu Linux profile.*

The Windows Terminal profiles that we cover in this chapter are available online at `https://github.com/PacktPublishing/Windows-Terminal-Tips-Tricks/tree/main/Chapter 14`.

Using Microsoft Azure's Cloud Shell and az interactive

In this section, we'll learn how to use Windows Terminal with Microsoft Azure, one of the top cloud providers used by many organizations, both on the Windows platform and beyond. Microsoft Azure has a generous **free tier** of 12 months, with some restrictions. In this section, we'll use free-tier resources when integrating Microsoft Azure into Windows Terminal.

Some of the work is already done for us; when we installed Windows Terminal, an **Azure Cloud Shell** profile was automatically created:

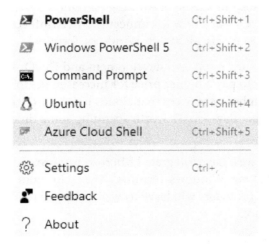

Figure 14.1 – Azure Cloud Shell available in Windows Terminal

If the **Azure Cloud Shell** menu option is not available in Windows Terminal, first ensure that it's not set to hidden (in Windows Terminal, find the **Azure Cloud Shell** profile and ensure `"hidden": true` is not set). The full profile definition is as follows:

```
{
  "guid": "{b453ae62-4e3d-5e58-b989-0a998ec441b8}",
  "name": "Azure Cloud Shell",
  "source": "Windows.Terminal.Azure"
}
```

The **Azure Cloud Shell** is a connection to a pre-configured **virtual machine** running in Microsoft Azure. By the end of this section, we'll be able to open a tab in Windows Terminal, seamlessly authenticate, and be dropped into our virtual machine running in the cloud. The best part is, Azure Cloud Shell can be accessed from anywhere! We can access it from Windows Terminal, the Microsoft Azure mobile app, or any browser by visiting `https://shell.azure.com`.

The Azure Cloud Shell comes with useful development tools out of the box, such as .NET, Python, and Node.js. It's also pre-loaded with tools for managing Azure **resources** such as virtual machines and storage devices.

When we first open Azure Cloud Shell, we'll be prompted to associate our terminal with our Microsoft Azure account, as seen in the following screenshot:

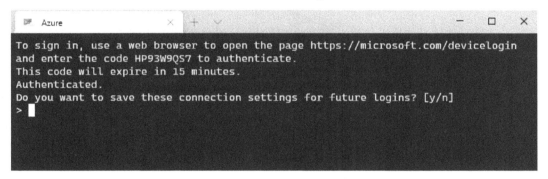

Figure 14.2 – Opening the Azure Cloud Shell menu item for the first time

After visiting `https://microsoft.com/devicelogin` and entering the authentication code, as per the on-screen instructions in Windows Terminal, we'll need to either log in or create a new Microsoft Azure account. For new accounts, a credit card is required for verification, but it won't be charged unless we upgrade to a paid account.

After we associate Windows Terminal with our Microsoft Azure account, we can provision a new Azure Cloud Shell instance by visiting `https://shell.azure.com`. We'll be presented with a choice of **Bash** or **PowerShell** (both on Linux). In this chapter, we'll select **PowerShell**, but the choice is not permanent; we can easily switch between the two:

Welcome to Azure Cloud Shell

Select Bash or PowerShell. You can change shells any time via the environment selector in the Cloud Shell toolbar. The most recently used environment will be the default for your next session.

Bash   PowerShell

Figure 14.3 – Selecting Bash or PowerShell on Linux for Azure Cloud Shell

Next, we'll be prompted to allocate some **storage** for our cloud shell. This storage is used to persist files across our Cloud Shell sessions. We can use our **Free Trial** subscription for this storage:

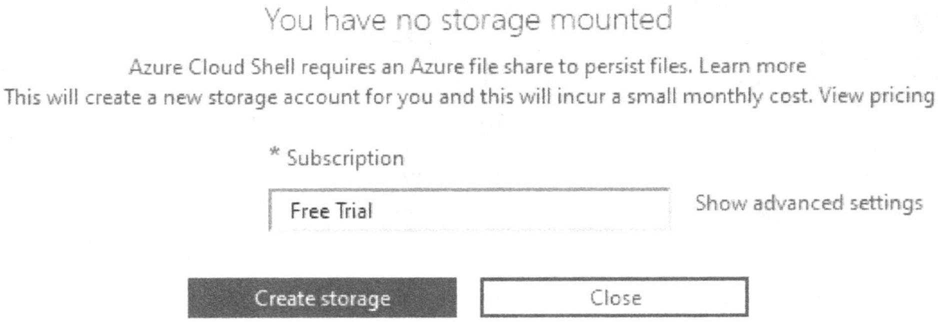

You have no storage mounted

Azure Cloud Shell requires an Azure file share to persist files. Learn more
This will create a new storage account for you and this will incur a small monthly cost. View pricing

* Subscription

| Free Trial | Show advanced settings

Create storage   Close

Figure 14.4 – Using our Free Trial subscription for our Cloud Shell storage

Now, when we open the **Azure** tab in Windows Terminal, we'll be able to access Cloud Shell in the Microsoft Azure cloud. We'll be prompted to select a **tenant ID** (**0** in the following screenshot):

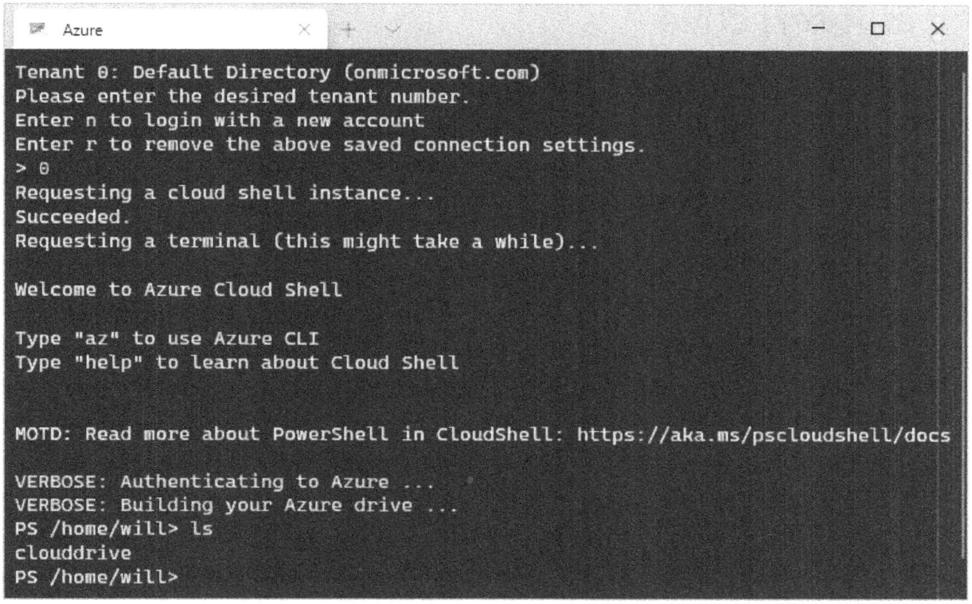

```
Tenant 0: Default Directory (onmicrosoft.com)
Please enter the desired tenant number.
Enter n to login with a new account
Enter r to remove the above saved connection settings.
> 0
Requesting a cloud shell instance...
Succeeded.
Requesting a terminal (this might take a while)...

Welcome to Azure Cloud Shell

Type "az" to use Azure CLI
Type "help" to learn about Cloud Shell


MOTD: Read more about PowerShell in CloudShell: https://aka.ms/pscloudshell/docs

VERBOSE: Authenticating to Azure ...
VERBOSE: Building your Azure drive ...
PS /home/will> ls
clouddrive
PS /home/will>
```

Figure 14.5 – Logging in to Cloud Shell in Windows Terminal

> **Note**
>
> A tenant in Microsoft Azure is conceptually like an organization; technically, it's an instance of **Azure Active Directory (AAD)** that controls the authentication of our user account(s). Free trial accounts will most likely only have a single tenant.

Now that we have Azure Cloud Shell set up, there's a wide range of activities we can do with it:

- Develop frontend and backend applications, as we've done in previous chapters. Azure Cloud Shell bundles .NET Core, Go, Java, Node.js, Python 2 and 3, MySQL, PostgreSQL, and much more.

- Transfer files by saving them to the `~/clouddrive` directory.

- Manage Azure resources using built-in Azure tools such as the `az` command and the **Azure PowerShell cmdlets**.

Let's look at this third activity in a bit more detail, with the `az interactive` command.

Using az interactive

The `az` command is one of the many tools bundled in Azure Cloud Shell. This command has subcommands for interacting with various Microsoft Azure services—at the last count, this was over 90 subcommands! Additionally, each subcommand has multiple additional subcommands and command-line flags.

It can be overwhelming to work with this many options in a command-line tool. Helpfully, one of the subcommands of `az` is the `az interactive` command.

The `az interactive` command provides a rich command-line interface for exploring the various operations available in Microsoft Azure. When we run `az interactive`, the command will perform some first-time setup, and then drop us into a command-line shell.

In this command-line shell, we can run the various `az` commands, and we'll get rich autocompletion, documentation, and examples in real time as we type, as shown in the following screenshot:

Figure 14.6 – The az interactive command displaying autocompletion and help documentation

When we run a command, it will return its response as JSON. For some types of commands, the JSON response can get quite large, so the `az interactive` shell provides some useful ways to filter this JSON. For example, let's run the `az account list-locations` command. This command will print out a list of the geographical locations available to our cloud subscription, with metadata about each location. The output is over 1,200 lines of JSON; let's use the `az interactive` shell to filter it to something understandable.

The `??JMESPath` syntax allows us to process the JSON returned by the last `az` command, according to the **JMESPath** specification available at `https://jmespath.org/`. For example, if we wanted to only show the names of the Azure locations, without the additional metadata, we could run the following two commands:

```
az account list-locations
?? [] .name
```

The first command returns the roughly 1,200 lines of JSON as an array. The second command uses the JMESPath syntax to access the `name` property of each element of the array.

As a more complex example, let's try to extract the latitude and longitude of each Microsoft Azure region. We can accomplish this with the following command:

```
?? [] .metadata. [latitude, longitude]
```

As shown in the following figure, we can see the JSON returned from the `az account list-locations` command, and then our command that filters it down to just the latitude/longitude data:

```
Azure
    "metadata": {
      "geographyGroup": "South America",
      "latitude": "-22.90278",
      "longitude": "-43.2075",
      "pairedRegion": [
        {
          "id": "/subscriptions/e8b6cddd-2ffa-4998-aa01-b01ebcb8becd/locations/brazilsouth",
          "name": "brazilsouth",
          "subscriptionId": null
        }
      ],
      "physicalLocation": "Rio",
      "regionCategory": "Other",
      "regionType": "Physical"
    },
    "name": "brazilsoutheast",
    "regionalDisplayName": "(South America) Brazil Southeast",
    "subscriptionId": null
  }
]
    ??[].metadata.[latitude,longitude]
[
  [
    "37.3719",
    "-79.8164"
  ],
  [
    "36.6681",
    "-78.3889"
  ],
```

Figure 14.7 – Top: the raw JSON output. Middle: our JMESPath filter. Bottom: the filtered JSON

While the JSON filtering helps with commands that return data about existing Microsoft Azure resources, `az` can also help with commands that modify resources. By using the `az find` command, we can find example usages of commands to better understand how they work before running them. For example, if we ran `az find storage`, we would get example commands that show the most common ways to use the `az storage` subcommand:

```
PS /home/will> az find storage
Finding examples...

Here are the most common ways to use [storage]:

Create a storage container in a storage account.
az storage container create --name mystoragecontainer

Delete blobs or files from Azure Storage. (autogenerated)
az storage remove --account-name myaccount --container-name MyContainer --only-show-errors --recursive

Remove all the blobs in a Storage Container.
az storage remove --container-name MyContainer --name path/to/directory
```

Figure 14.8 – The output of az find storage, which shows how to use various storage commands

Sometimes it feels like half of running cloud commands is searching the web for examples beforehand; this `az find` command helps us stay in our terminal for a more streamlined workflow.

We are lucky that Azure Cloud Shell is already part of Windows Terminal; it provides a fast and easy way to get up and running. In the following sections, we'll look at how to add similar support for other clouds. First up: Google Cloud.

Using Google Cloud Shell and gcloud interactive

In this section, we'll see how to use Windows Terminal with Google Cloud. Google Cloud is decidedly more "Linux-oriented" than Microsoft Azure; while it's definitely possible and supported to use Windows, some operations are just easier on Linux. For this reason, we'll be using the WSL2 installation that we set up previously in *Chapter 3, Configuring an Ubuntu Linux profile*.

Like Microsoft Azure, Google Cloud supports both a cloud shell and rich command-line tools for managing resources. Google Cloud Shell is a virtual machine running in Google Cloud, with common tools and languages pre-installed. It contains the programming language runtimes for .NET Core, Java, Go, Python 2 and 3, Node.js, Ruby, and PHP, and other tools such as TensorFlow and Docker are pre-installed as well. It can be accessed from Windows Terminal, the Google Cloud Console mobile app, and online at `https://shell.cloud.google.com`.

Before we can start using Google Cloud Shell, we'll need to do a bit of setup work:

1. We'll need a Google Cloud account, which includes a free trial with $300 worth of credit. Create an account at `https://cloud.google.com/`, following the on-screen instructions.

2. Next, we'll install the **Google Cloud SDK** into our WSL2 installation following the instructions at `https://cloud.google.com/sdk/`. The instructions for Ubuntu involve adding the Google Cloud package repository and installing the `google-cloud-sdk` package using `apt`.

3. Finally, run the `gcloud init` command to associate our WSL2 installation with our Google Cloud account. This command will generate a sign-in URL, which we can open by holding the *Ctrl* key while clicking the URL in Windows Terminal. After successfully signing in, we can copy the verification code back into our terminal to complete the association.

After our terminal is associated with our Google Cloud account, we'll be prompted to create a **Cloud project**. We can enter any project name here, but it needs to be globally unique across Google Cloud; for example, test-project won't work, but test-project-11235813 may.

Now that we're all set up, we can launch Google Cloud Shell with the following command:

```
gcloud beta cloud-shell ssh --authorize-session
```

This command will start our Cloud Shell virtual machine, generate a ~/.ssh/google_compute_engine public/private key pair, and connect to the machine using SSH.

To avoid needing to memorize the previous command, we can add it as a menu entry in Windows Terminal! In the settings.json file (*Ctrl + Shift + ,*), we can add the following profile. Remember, the actual value of the "guid" field doesn't matter, as long as it's unique:

```
{
    "guid": "{1e1d2e8f-a96a-4ba4-9580-fb1ede564367}",
    "name": "Google Cloud Shell",
    "commandline": "wsl.exe gcloud beta cloud-shell ssh
--authorize-session",
}
```

Now, we have a shell accessible from anywhere, whether it's in a browser, on our mobile phone, or in Windows Terminal. We can use this cloud shell for frontend or backend development, transferring files between computers, and administering resources in Google Cloud. Let's look at how we might administer Google Cloud resources next.

Using gcloud beta interactive

Just like Azure's az interactive command, Google Cloud supports an interactive shell, currently in beta. Running the gcloud interactive command will redirect us to run either gcloud alpha interactive or gcloud beta interactive. We'll be using gcloud beta interactive for a more stable experience; it's possible that in the future we'll no longer need to include the beta keyword.

When we run gcloud beta interactive, we get a command-line shell that adds autocompletion and help documentation as we type commands:

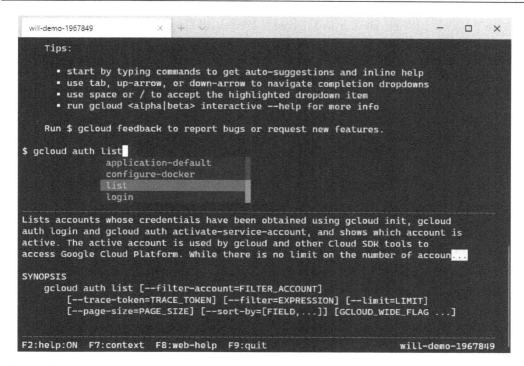

Figure 14.9 – The gcloud beta interactive command provides autocompletion and help documentation

This `gcloud interactive` shell provides autocompletion and documentation not only for `gcloud` commands but also for any command that has man page documentation. This means we don't need to switch between our `gcloud interactive` shell and our normal Linux shell; we can run normal shell commands right inside our `gcloud interactive` shell.

Using Google Cloud Shell in Windows Terminal, as well as the `gcloud beta interactive` command, gives us convenient and fast access to Google Cloud from Windows Terminal.

We've now learned how to integrate both Microsoft Azure and Google Cloud into Windows Terminal. There's one major cloud provider we haven't yet discussed, and it's the big one: AWS.

Using AWS from Windows Terminal

In this section, we'll set up an AWS account, experiment with the `aws-shell` command-line UI, and explore the AWS Tools for PowerShell.

AWS also has a cloud shell, similar to Microsoft Azure and Google Cloud. Unfortunately, **AWS CloudShell** is browser-only for now and does not yet expose a programmatic interface that we can use to integrate it into Windows Terminal. As we can only use it from the browser, we won't be covering it in this book. Instead, we'll cover several useful command-line tools.

Before we get started, we'll need to create a free AWS account and generate some AWS access keys; our tools will use these access keys to interact with the AWS API on our behalf:

1. Sign up for an AWS account at `https://aws.amazon.com/`.

2. After the account is created, navigate to the AWS Console.

3. Go to the top-right account menu, as shown in *Figure 14.10*, and select **My Security Credentials**.

4. Generate new access keys. This will create both an **access key ID** and a **secret access key**. Store these keys somewhere safe:

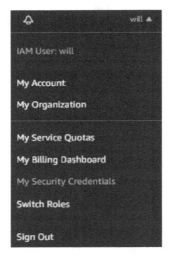

Figure 14.10 – Accessing My Security Credentials to generate AWS access keys

Now that we have our access keys, let's set up `aws-shell` so we can conveniently manage AWS resources from Windows Terminal.

Using aws-shell

`aws-shell`, released by AWS labs, is a rich command-line shell with built-in autocompletion and help documentation. It's very similar to the previous interactive commands we learned about for Microsoft Azure and Google Cloud:

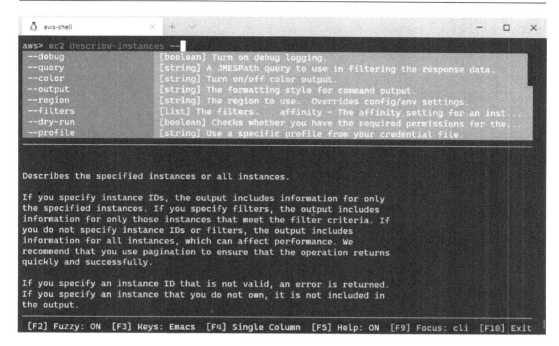

Figure 14.11 – aws-shell showing autocompletion and help documentation

aws-shell runs best on Linux, so we'll again be installing it in WSL2:

1. Open a **WSL2** tab in Windows Terminal and run the following command:

    ```
    sudo pip3 install aws-shell
    ```

2. Once the installation is complete, run the aws-shell command.

3. Inside aws-shell, run the configure command, and enter the AWS access keys we generated previously.

Like the Microsoft Azure shell, aws-shell returns JSON output. We can use JMESPath (https://jmespath.org/) to filter this JSON into something more understandable by using the --query command-line flag. For example, we can run the following command to get a list of all AWS geographical regions, and then filter it down to only the region names:

```
ec2 describe-regions --query "Regions[].RegionName"
```

The result can be seen in the following screenshot:

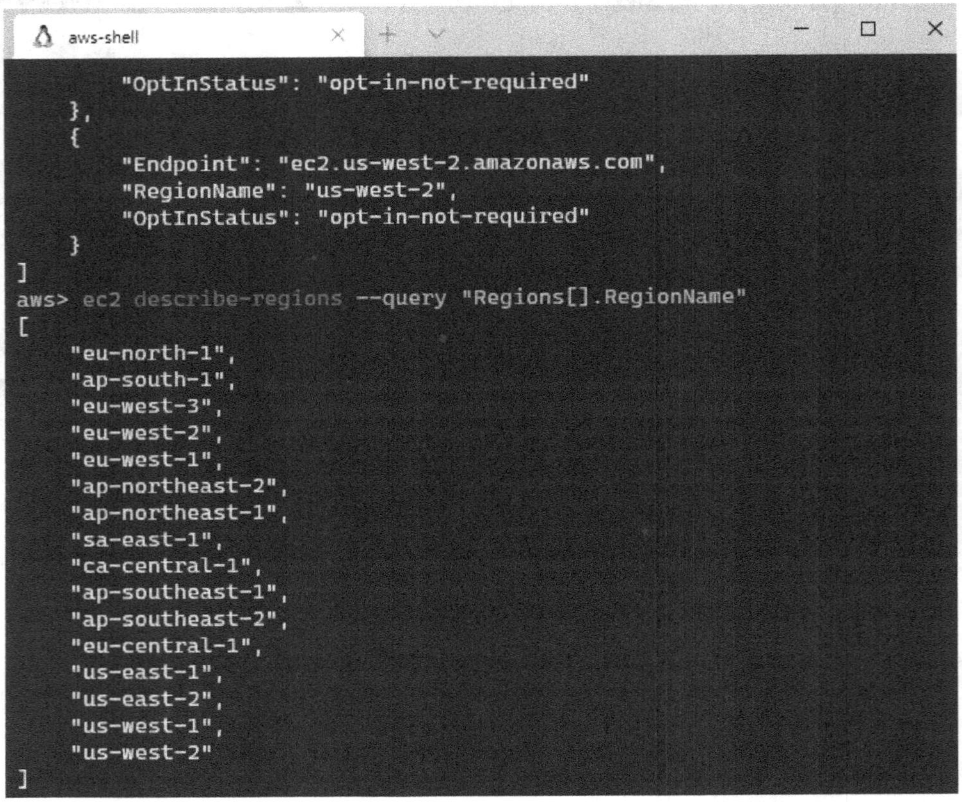

```
"OptInStatus": "opt-in-not-required"
        },
        {
            "Endpoint": "ec2.us-west-2.amazonaws.com",
            "RegionName": "us-west-2",
            "OptInStatus": "opt-in-not-required"
        }
    ]
aws> ec2 describe-regions --query "Regions[].RegionName"
    [
        "eu-north-1",
        "ap-south-1",
        "eu-west-3",
        "eu-west-2",
        "eu-west-1",
        "ap-northeast-2",
        "ap-northeast-1",
        "sa-east-1",
        "ca-central-1",
        "ap-southeast-1",
        "ap-southeast-2",
        "eu-central-1",
        "us-east-1",
        "us-east-2",
        "us-west-1",
        "us-west-2"
    ]
```

Figure 14.12 – Using JMESPath parameters to filter JSON returned by AWS commands

Notice that we don't need to prefix each command with aws; they're prefixed with aws automatically for us. This is often what we want, but it's also possible to run shell commands such as ls from inside aws-shell, in a couple of different ways:

- For most commands, we simply prefix the command with an exclamation point; for example, !ls will run the ls shell command.

- To change the current working directory of aws-shell, we can use the .cd command (it's prefixed with a period).

- Finally, we can pipe the JSON output of any command to a shell command—anything after the pipe character (|) is assumed to be a shell command. For example, ec2 describe-instances | grep production would search the JSON output for the word production.

The final convenience of aws-shell is its autocompletion capabilities. For certain commands that take IDs of AWS resources, we can use tab completion to complete these IDs. For example, if we wanted to start an EC2 instance with the i-a5e9a33f0 instance ID, aws-shell can tab-complete this instance ID as part of the ec2 start-instances command.

As our last step, let's add the AWS shell to Windows Terminal with the following profile definition:

```
{
    "guid": "{c2c1e634-6539-4b1c-aa2b-9632f122602a}",
    "name": "AWS Shell",
    "commandline": "wsl.exe aws-shell"
}
```

Now, when we need to interact with AWS services, we can enter aws-shell at the press of a button, without needing to click through the AWS Console in our browser.

Using the AWS Tools for PowerShell

If we don't want to use WSL2 for our AWS management, we can use the **AWS Tools for PowerShell**, a set of PowerShell modules released by Amazon. These PowerShell modules map closely to the AWS API, using the familiar Verb-Noun naming conventions common to PowerShell modules. The command-line experience is not as integrated as aws-shell, but its adherence to the PowerShell conventions can make it more intuitive for those already at home in PowerShell.

As the AWS API is quite large, the PowerShell modules can be optionally split into smaller, service-specific modules, so we only need to download and import our required functionality. There is a bundled option available as well, which includes all available modules in a single download. We'll be using this bundled version to avoid needing to download many different modules. Information about both the bundled version and the modular version can be found at https://aws.amazon.com/powershell/.

To install the bundled version, we can run the following command from a PowerShell profile in Windows Terminal:

```
Install-Module -Name AWSPowerShell.NetCore
```

This will download and install the PowerShell module. After it's complete, we can save our AWS access keys as the default keys for future AWS API operations:

```
Import-Module AWSPowerShell.NetCore
Set-AWSCredential -AccessKey <access-key> -SecretKey <secret-key> -StoreAs default
```

Now, we can access all AWS resources via PowerShell. For example, if we wanted to get a list of all running EC2 virtual machines in our account, we could use the `Get-Ec2Instances` command:

```
Get-EC2Instance -Filter @{Name = "instance-state-name"; Value = "running"}
```

This will return a PowerShell array that represents our EC2 instances. We can then use our standard PowerShell cmdlets for manipulating this array, such as `ForEach-Object` or `Where-Object`. We can even pipe the results of one AWS command to another, to build up chains of commands for complex AWS operations.

By using the AWS Tools for PowerShell or `aws-shell` (or a combination of both!), we don't need to navigate back and forth in our browser to manage our cloud resources. Instead, we can use Windows Terminal to make AWS management operations straightforward, repeatable, and predictable.

Summary

In this chapter, we covered how to use Windows Terminal with the three most popular cloud-based systems. We covered Microsoft Azure's Cloud Shell and the `az` command, especially focusing on using `az interactive` to get instant feedback on our commands.

Next, we looked at Google Cloud, which also supports a cloud shell and a `gcloud beta interactive` command for quickly manipulating Google Cloud resources.

Finally, we covered AWS. We used the `aws-shell` command, a convenient way of interacting with resources in AWS, as well as the AWS Tools for PowerShell.

Appendix
Windows Terminal
Actions

We covered a subset of Windows Terminal actions in both *Chapter 6*, *Setting up keyboard shortcuts*, and *Chapter 7*, *Hidden Windows Terminal Actions*. This *Appendix* lists all the actions that are available as of Windows Terminal 1.6.

As a reminder, the syntax for binding a Windows Terminal action to a keyboard shortcut is as follows:

```
{
  "command": {
    "action": "actionName",
    "property": "value"
  },
  "keys": "keyboard+shortcut"
}
```

Here, `property` is one or more unique properties that belong to the action. Let's look at an example:

```
{
  "command": {
    "action": "splitPane",
    "split": "auto"
  },
  "keys": "alt+shift+d"
}
```

In this example, the `split` property can only be used with the `"splitPane"` action. If the action does not require any properties, or we want all the properties to use their default values, the following shorthand can be used. It is equivalent to the previous example because the default value of the `split` property is `"auto"`.

```
{
  "command": "splitPane",
  "keys": "alt+shift+d"
}
```

Additionally, we can provide a `name` property and omit the `keys` property if we only intend to use the action via the Command Palette. An `icon` property will specify the icon to show in the Command Palette.

List of Windows Terminal actions

adjustFontSize – Increases or decreases the font size. It takes a required integer `delta` property that represents how much to change the size by, in points.

closeOtherTabs – Closes all tabs except one. It takes an optional integer `index` property that specifies which tab to keep open. If omitted, it uses the currently active tab.

closePane – Closes the current pane. It does not take any properties.

closeTab – Closes the current tab. It does not take any properties.

closeTabsAfter – Closes all tabs after the specified tab. It takes an optional integer `index` property that specifies the tab. If omitted, it uses the currently active tab.

closeWindow – Closes the current window. It does not take any properties.

commandPalette – Opens the command palette. It takes an optional string `launchMode` property that can contain either `"action"` or `"commandLine"`. The value `"action"` is the default and will configure the command palette to accept Windows Terminal actions. The value `"commandLine"` configures the command palette to accept `wt` commands, such as `"split-pane"`. It can also accept shell commands.

copy – Copies text to the clipboard. It takes an optional boolean `singleLine` property that specifies whether or not newlines are removed from the copied content. It also takes an optional `copyFormatting` property that controls how formatting (font colors and styles) is copied. `copyFormatting` can be a string array of `["html", "rtf"]`; a boolean that, if true, will copy both HTML and RTF; or the strings `"html"`, `"rtf"`, `"all"`, or `"none"`. This requires the application that the text is being pasted into to support these formats (such as Microsoft Word).

duplicateTab – Duplicates the current tab. It does not take any properties. This will respect OSC 9;9 messages for setting the current working directory, as discussed in *Chapter 5, Changing your Windows Terminal appearance*.

find – Opens the search box. It does not take any properties.

findMatch – Finds the next or previous occurrence of the text that was last searched for in the search box. It takes an optional string direction property that can contain either "next" or "prev", with "prev" being the default.

moveFocus – Moves focus between panes. It takes an optional string direction property that can contain "left", "right", "up", "down", or "previous". The default is "left".

moveTab – Moves the current tab in the tab UI. It takes a required string direction property that can contain either "forward" or "backward".

newTab – Opens a new tab. It takes optional properties that can be used to configure the shell that opens in the new tab. The string profile property can be either the GUID or name of the profile to launch, or the integer index property specifies the index of the profile in the settings to launch. If neither of these properties is set, the default profile is launched. The string commandline, tabTitle, tabColor, and startingDirectory properties will override their corresponding properties in the launched profile's configuration.

newWindow – Opens a new window. It takes the same properties as newTab.

nextTab – Navigates to the next tab (to the right). It does not take any properties.

openNewTabDropdown – Opens the drop-down menu in the Windows Terminal UI, where a new tab or pane can be launched. It does not take any properties.

openSettings – Opens the settings for Windows Terminal. It takes a string target property that controls which settings page to open. It can contain "settingsFile", "defaultsFile", "allFiles", or "settingsUI".

openTabColorPicker – Opens a color picker that can be used to change the current tab's color. It does not take any properties.

openTabRenamer – Opens a text field that can be used to change the current tab's title. It does not take any properties.

paste – Pastes the current contents of the clipboard. It does not take any properties.

prevTab – Navigates to the previous tab (to the left). It does not take any properties.

renameTab – Changes the current tab's title. It takes an optional string `title` property that specifies the title to use. If omitted, it reverts the tab's title to the default.

resetFontSize – Resets the current font size to the default. It does not take any properties.

resizePane – Changes the active pane's size. It takes an optional string `direction` property that specifies the direction of the resize. It can contain `"left"`, `"right"`, `"up"`, or `"down"`.

scrollUp and **scrollDown** – Scrolls the terminal up or down by a number of rows. It takes an optional integer `rowsToScroll` property, and if this is omitted it uses the system's default value.

scrollUpPage and **scrollDownPage** – Scrolls the terminal up or down by the height of one screen. It does not take any properties.

scrollToTop and **scrollToBottom** – Scrolls the terminal all the way to the top or bottom of the input buffer. It does not take any properties.

sendInput – Inputs text as if typed into the terminal. It takes a string `input` property of the text to send. This text supports pressing *Enter* by using the escape sequence `\n`, and also supports ANSI escape sequences for emulating key presses such as the arrow keys.

setColorScheme – Sets the color scheme of the currently selected pane. It takes a required string `colorScheme` property that contains the name of `colorScheme`.

setTabColor – Sets the current tab's color. It takes an optional string `color` property that specifies an RGB color of the format `"#FFFFFF"` or `"#FFF"`. If omitted, it resets back to the default tab color.

splitPane – Opens a new pane in the current tab. It takes the optional properties covered in the earlier `newTab` command that control the profile to open. In addition, it takes an optional string `split` property that can be `"horizontal"`, `"vertical"` or `"auto"` (which tries to keep the most square pane size). It takes an optional decimal `size` property that represents the initial size of the pane, as a fraction of the current pane (for example, 0.5). It takes a `splitMode` property that currently must be the value `"duplicate"`.

switchToTab – Switches to the specified tab. It takes an optional integer `index` that starts at index 0. If omitted, 0 is the default.

tabSearch – Opens the "tab search" UI that can search all open tabs' title text, and navigate to the matching tab. It does not take any properties.

toggleAlwaysOnTop – Pins and unpins Windows Terminal on top of all other windows, so it will not be sent behind other windows when those windows receive focus. It does not take any properties.

toggleFocusMode – Hides and shows Windows Terminal's UI components, so only the shell is displayed (all tabs and the Windows title bar are hidden. It does not take any properties.

toggleFullscreen – Enters and exits full-screen mode, so Windows Terminal fully fills the screen. It does not take any properties.

togglePaneZoom – Temporarily makes the current pane fully fill the Windows Terminal, so other other panes are hidden. It does not take any properties.

toggleReadOnlyMode – Enters and exits read-only mode for the current pane, so it will not accept user input and shows a confirmation when closed. It does not take any properties.

toggleShaderEffects – Enables and disables the pixel shader specified by the `experimental.pixelShaderPath` property in the current profile. It does not take any properties.

wt – Executes a `wt` command line in Windows Terminal. Takes a string `commandline` property, which can be a single command or a set of semicolon-delimited commands such as `"split-pane"`, `"new-tab"`, or `"focus-tab"`.

Packt.com

Subscribe to our online digital library for full access to over 7,000 books and videos, as well as industry leading tools to help you plan your personal development and advance your career. For more information, please visit our website.

Why subscribe?

- Spend less time learning and more time coding with practical eBooks and Videos from over 4,000 industry professionals

- Improve your learning with Skill Plans built especially for you

- Get a free eBook or video every month

- Fully searchable for easy access to vital information

- Copy and paste, print, and bookmark content

Did you know that Packt offers eBook versions of every book published, with PDF and ePub files available? You can upgrade to the eBook version at packt.com and as a print book customer, you are entitled to a discount on the eBook copy. Get in touch with us at customercare@packtpub.com for more details.

At www.packt.com, you can also read a collection of free technical articles, sign up for a range of free newsletters, and receive exclusive discounts and offers on Packt books and eBooks.

Other Books You May Enjoy

If you enjoyed this book, you may be interested in these other books by Packt:

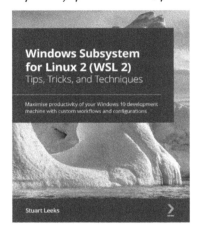

Windows Subsystem for Linux 2 (WSL 2) Tips, Tricks, and Techniques

Stuart Leeks

ISBN: 978-1-80056-244-8

- Install and configure Windows Subsystem for Linux and Linux distros
- Access web applications running in Linux from Windows
- Invoke Windows applications, file systems, and environment variables from bash in WSL
- Customize the appearance and behavior of the Windows Terminal to suit your preferences and workflows
- Explore various tips for enhancing the Visual Studio Code experience with WSL
- Install and work with Docker and Kubernetes within Windows Subsystem for Linux
- Discover various productivity tips for working with Command-line tools in WSL

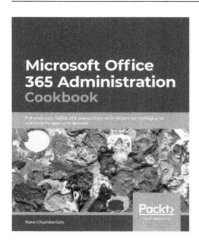

Microsoft Office 365 Administration Cookbook

Nate Chamberlain

ISBN: 978-1-83855-123-0

- Get to grips with basic Office 365 setup and routine administration tasks
- Manage Office 365 identities and groups efficiently and securely
- Harness the capabilities of PowerShell to automate common administrative tasks
- Configure and manage core Office 365 services such as Exchange Online, SharePoint, and OneDrive
- Configure and administer fast-evolving services such as Microsoft Search, Power Platform, Microsoft Teams, and Azure AD
- Get up and running with advanced threat protection features provided by the Microsoft 365 Security & Compliance Center
- Protect your organization's sensitive data with Office 365 Data Loss Prevention
- Monitor activities and behaviors across all Office 365 services

Packt is searching for authors like you

If you're interested in becoming an author for Packt, please visit `authors.packtpub.com` and apply today. We have worked with thousands of developers and tech professionals, just like you, to help them share their insight with the global tech community. You can make a general application, apply for a specific hot topic that we are recruiting an author for, or submit your own idea.

Leave a review - let other readers know what you think

Please share your thoughts on this book with others by leaving a review on the site that you bought it from. If you purchased the book from Amazon, please leave us an honest review on this book's Amazon page. This is vital so that other potential readers can see and use your unbiased opinion to make purchasing decisions, we can understand what our customers think about our products, and our authors can see your feedback on the title that they have worked with Packt to create. It will only take a few minutes of your time, but is valuable to other potential customers, our authors, and Packt. Thank you!

Index

www.ingramcontent.com/pod-product-compliance
Lightning Source LLC
Chambersburg PA
CBHW060540060326
40690CB00017B/3551